Welsh Choirs
on Tour

For Peg and Mal,
aka Mam and Dad, and our family –
thanks for everything.

To Jen and my other family.
I hope you mostly enjoyed the ride.
Thanks for being there.

Welsh Choirs
on Tour

What goes on tour,
stays on tour... or does it?

Alan Maggs

with Peter Read

First impression: 2014

The publishers wish to acknowledge the support of
Cyngor Llyfrau Cymru

Cover illustration: Tony Kelly

ISBN: 978 184771 691 0

Published and printed in Wales
on paper from well-maintained forests by
Y Lolfa Cyf., Talybont, Ceredigion SY24 5HE
website www.ylolfa.com
e-mail ylolfa@ylolfa.com
tel 01970 832 304
fax 832 782

Contents

Acknowledgements   6

Introduction   7

1   The Choir Trip   9

2   Alfonso's Tale   42

3   Is Wales in Africa?   45

    Joke from the Coach I   57

4   Lost in Translation   58

5   Every Choir has its Characters   73

6   What the Average Male Voice
Chorister Knows about Women   97

7   Choir Practice   98

    Joke from the Coach II   105

8   Not Just a Choir, More a Way of Life   107

9   Sinning with the Choir   121

10   On a Personal Note   130

    Joke from the Coach III   139

Acknowledgements

*A*BRAZOS A GRAHAM *y Dori, Jarmo y Anka – gracias por su ayuda y amistad en España.*

Thank you Peter for your initial encouragement and for your support in writing this book.

Thank you to all who kindly provided photographs. Thanks for the memories.

Special thanks to all the choirs which have had to put up with me over the past 20 years. You know who you are!

Introduction

I WAS BORN in the late 1950s and raised in a mining village at a time when Wales still had mining communities. For the first 14 years of my life I was frogmarched to choir practice at the local chapel. At 14 my family moved to Swansea. My voice broke overnight. Must have been the sea air but at least I was no longer required by a choir. Any choir!

Fast forward 20 years and I found myself in a Spanish bar, in a typical Spanish town. The conversation centred on the town's choral heritage and, fortified by the local brew, I said something like: "You can't claim to be a musical town until you've received a visit from a Welsh choir."

"Well, bring one to us," said the tall distinguished Spaniard who, unknown to me, was the town's councillor for culture... and so I did.

In fact over the next 20 years I helped organise scores of trips for choirs to that particular town and scores more to various parts of Europe and the UK. Many of which, I accompanied. This book is an affectionate tribute to some of the very many characters I got to know in often quite surreal situations.

Of course as befits a book about culture (?), a certain amount of poetic licence has been employed and certain names have been changed to save embarrassment, including mine in at least one story.

I hope you enjoy the book... I am sure you'll recognise some of the characters.

Alan Maggs
February 2014

CHAPTER 1

The Choir Trip

E D WAS A happy man. Recently divorced from Mavis, he was going on tour with the choir. His ex-wife, Mavis, never liked travelling abroad, so Ed hadn't been to the continent since his disastrous honeymoon in Benidorm. That was two adult children and 24 years ago, so he wasn't too disappointed when Mavis took up with Clive, the camper van man who lived next door. Although he wished the couple no harm, he was hoping the heavens might open and chuck it down on their camping trip to the Brecon Beacons. Anyway, he was with his butties from the choir and they were heading for Spain! Five days on the Costa Blanca, two concerts, plenty of sun, sea, sangria and socialising, this was his first trip abroad since that disaster of a honeymoon and, along with his mates, Ed was determined to make the most of it.

Choir suit, shoes, shirt, tie and polo shirt packed, along with an assortment of Man at C&A shorts and T-shirts, colourful Hawaiian-style shirts, summer slacks, white socks and a selection of Y-fronts and boxers, along with an abundance of shampoos, shower gels, sun-creams, deodorants, aftershave lotions and potions, Ed joined his mates at the Rec car park, and waited for the bus to take them to the airport. Of course, with 40 choristers waiting in the car park and the club closed, the bus was always going to be late. And it was at this moment that Ed got his wish – the heavens opened and chucked it down. No doubt the sun was shining in Brecon.

Mike, the regular bus driver, apologised for being late, but the new bus was a touch higher than the usual one and struggled to get under the old bridge into town. This meant a detour which unfortunately took Mike via the bacon sandwich van – and we all know about bus drivers and sandwich vans.

Of course, there was no sign of rain when Mike pulled into the lay-by for his bacon sandwich and hot tea. When the first large drop plopped into his scalding hot drink and the second and third landed on the remains of his sandwich, he knew the guys would be getting wet. Mike leapt into action. Weighing-in at 19 stone, 'leapt' is a bit of an exaggeration, but he did move.

As the heavens opened, Jeff pulled into the car park in his £45,000 motor, driven by his new, youngish model wife. Jeff was the choir's 'wealthy bugger' who had made a fortune from building and having his fingers in several profitable pies.

"'Ere, look at that motor," said Big Bri.

"Must be worth £50,000."

"£45,000 and change," Arwyn corrected Bri.

"£45,000, that's more than my house is worth," said Phil, the not so successful builder.

"Yes but he works in London a lot and you can't speed up the motorway in your house," said Arwyn.

"True" said Phil, "but nor can you have a crap and a bath in his motor!"

The boys were a bit damp but still in good humour when Mike pulled into the car park only ten minutes late. Unfortunately, loading luggage and getting 40 people on the bus always seems to take longer when it's raining and everyone is getting soaked. Worse, the boys would have to wear the wet clothes for the rest of the day until they arrived at the hotel and could change into their 'summer clothes'. A point the already sniffling and spluttering Harold, choir hypochondriac, was quick to point out between sneezes. There was a decision to be made for Harold. Harold had to sit in the front of the bus otherwise he would come over "all queasy like – travel sick see – I 'as got to see where I is going". Unfortunately, the now ever so slightly damp Harold also wanted to sit next to a heater so that he could dry out before his "pneumonia kicked in like". This second option was academic as Mike hadn't yet worked out how to operate the heaters on the new bus!

When travelling any distance the last thing you want is to sit next to someone for whom the words bath and deodorant are distant memories. A lovely bloke, Trev. Salt of the earth. Will do anything for anyone... except perhaps take a regular shower.

New to the choir, nervous traveller and youngest member Layton had grabbed a window seat where he hoped he could spend the bus journey undisturbed, staring blankly at the view as it sped past. Twenty stone of unwashed and sweaty Trev was not what nervous Layton needed as he struggled to ease his way into his first trip with the choir.

As the last on to the bus, and therefore the wettest, Trev's latest encounter with water for the first time in several days hadn't improved his aroma. As Trev settled in next to Layton, the combination of damp clothes, sweat, eau de carbolic spray, and the freshly opened can of Strongbow was almost more than the frail and nervous Layton could bear. And they hadn't left the car park yet! As Trev offered Layton a pork pie and a can of cider and Mike started to ease his new bus out of the car park, Layton shrieked, "I got to get off – I'm going to be sick". Mike stopped the bus and Layton sprinted to the bins at the back of the club where the contents of his stomach soon found their way to his brand new trainers.

"Uncle Dai, he is your family. Go after 'im and get 'im back on the bus. He can sit up front next to me," said helpful, Hypochondriac Harold.

"Some f***ing incentive that," muttered Dai, "and I is not 'is uncle. I do sometimes escort his mam to bingo and occasionally take 'er out for a bit now that Brenda from the social 'as nabbed 'is dad, and they 'ave buggered off to Cwmbrân."

"Bit of wot? Dirty bugger," chorused the back seat!

"Dirty lucky bugger," said Bri. "Layton's mam is tidy like."

Layton was force fed a shed-load of mints and shoved back on the bus by a none too sympathetic 'Uncle' Dai.

"Here, sit next to Hypo Harold, he'll look after you."

"I am not a hypochondriac," said Hypo. "Sit by 'ere good boy. You want a travel sickness pill?"

For the second time that day Mike had forgotten the height of his new chariot and, as he pulled out of the car park, the scrunch of metal on stone and the sudden disappearance of his wing mirror alerted him to the fact that those extra couple of inches can make all the difference. Something Mike had pondered for most of his adult life.

The offending wing mirror was still attached to the bus but was hanging limply to the side of the vehicle. "Layton climb up on Big Bri's shoulders and see if you can get the mirror off," said Arwyn.

"Why me?" asked Layton as he noticed the remnants of last night's pizza on his trainers "Look at the state of my new trainers. Why is it that whenever you throw up, there always seems to be carrots? I hate carrots. So why is there carrots on my trainers?" he asked his new neighbour Hypo Harold.

Hypo was now feeling a bit sick himself. Perhaps he didn't like carrots either.

"'Cos you is young and fit enough to get up there," explained Arwyn "and light enough for Bri to hold you. Pass Layton the hammer."

"Whoa, boys," Mike intervened, suddenly visualising his boss's face as he tried to explain why thousands of pounds worth of bus had been attacked by a hammer wielding chorister.

"Sorry boys – can't travel without a wing mirror. It's more

than my job's worth. I'll have to phone the depot and get a replacement coach here. Won't be long and we've allowed plenty of time to get you lot to the airport. No way am I going to let you miss your flight. I can do with a few days away from your whingeing and whining, so I'll make sure you get on the plane. Don't drink too much now boys. We won't be long getting a replacement bus and there's no toil..."

The last part of Mike's announcement was lost on some of the choir. They'd spotted that Barry, the not so genial mein host of the club, was opening up. Those at the back slipped off first to beat the inevitable crush at the bar.

On a good day, Barry looked like a bulldog chewing a wasp. "Wot you lot doing here? I deliberately opened up late today, hoping you'd 'ave buggered off already."

"We 'as been 'ere an hour an' we 'aven't left the bloody car park yet. Bloody great start," said Chairman Bill.

"Don't worry boys," said Arwyn, the long suffering choir sec and tour organiser. "We have allowed for this. We were starting off two hours earlier than necessary so we could get to a pub near the airport and have a few before getting on the plane. No worries, we'll be on the aeroplane."

True to his word Mike's call for a replacement bus was swiftly answered and their new vehicle arrived just as the first boys at the bar were considering a second pint.

"By the time they switch the luggage over we can shift a quick one," said Uncle Dai – not for a second considering that his case was one of those that had to be shifted and perhaps he should shift it himself. "Maybe we should get a few take-outs," said ideas man Bob.

At last the choir was on its way, with Mike, now in his familiar vehicle, having safely negotiated the car park gates. Five minutes into the journey Mike wound up the choir by playing the CD of their bitter local rivals from the next valley. To hoots of derision, Mike explained that he thought they might be inspired by this obvious touch of class.

Twenty minutes into the journey came a shout, or was it a plea, from the back of the bus.

"Where's the toilet, Mike, I'm busting?"

"Toilet, what toilet? I told you as you were getting off the other bus not to drink too much as there's no toilet on this one," said Mike.

"Didn't hear that," was the chorus from the back seat.

"Try and hold it boys and I'll pull into the services up the road, but if we have to stop again there'll be no time for the pub!"

Arwyn grabs the microphone. "Boys bach, come on, get it sorted. I'm not getting on the plane without a couple of pints so we'd better make the pub and I have a feeling young Layton feels the same."

By now, young Layton, although fortified by Hypo's travel sickness pills and a can of Trev's cider, had lost the will to live. Hypo had taken Layton under his wing and was regaling him with tales of turbulence and blow outs (on motorways, on runways and in bathrooms), of sciatica, in-growing toenails and burst appendix. When the choir pulled into the services Layton stayed on the bus. His young bladder not yet in desperate need of the toilet, he thought his time away from Hypo Harold would be better spent raiding Trev's cider stash... and another of Hypo's pills wouldn't hurt.

To the sound of cheers, Mike reminded the boys that it was straight on to the pub, no stopping.

The call came about 20 minutes later, "How long to the pub Mike?"

Fifteen minutes later, "Are we there yet?" to which, and in a surprisingly calm manner, Mike responded, "No, we are not there yet. If we were, the bus would be parked outside the pub and not hurtling up the motorway. Bloody daft question!"

Not unusually, Arwyn frowned. It puzzled him how certain members of the choir constantly set low personal standards and then failed to achieve them. Ten minutes later he had to intervene.

"Mike, we have to stop. Some of the boys will never make it to the pub."

"Sorry Arwyn," said Mike, "it's pub or services. We don't have time to stop at both. Rules are rules and I have to stop for 45 minutes somewhere. We won't have time to stop twice. Put it to the vote."

And so it was that the bus pulled into the services. For once the ageing bladders sensibly won over the craving for beer. Arwyn joined Layton and raided Trev's cider stash. Trev didn't mind. He was a good man, generous to a fault, despite being a bit smelly. And so our intrepid travellers reached the airport and somehow managed to find their check-in desk. It wasn't difficult to find. They were a bit late and there was a queue. Ed and his mates were about tenth in line and amongst the first of the choir. Happy at being at the airport at last and soon to be well and truly on the plane to Spain, Ed smiled at the check-in girl.

"Passport, sir."

"Thank you, luv, but I already have one," said Ed. In no way was he trying to be funny.

"No sir, that wasn't an enquiry, I need to check your passport."

A naive traveller and thinking his mates were somehow winding him up, Ed grinned inanely at the check-in girl. His mates assured him that this was no wind up and offered their own passports as proof.

"Come on, Ed. What's going on? I'm desperate for a slash," said a baritone as Ed announced that he did indeed have a passport and that, as instructed by Arwyn, he had kept it safe. So safe in fact that he had packed it in his suitcase! "Perhaps you could open your suitcase sir and retrieve it for me," said patient check-in girl, pointing to the black and battered suitcase in front of Eddie.

15

"That's not my case," said Ed. "This is his case," pointing to his mate, Berwyn. "That's my case," said Ed, pointing at his new Debenhams' 50 per cent sale special that, having been mistakenly checked-in, was just about to disappear over the edge of the carousel! Check-in girl reacted quickly and pressed the carousel STOP button. Ed's case teetered on the brink and hung there for what seemed an age – a bit like the bus at the end of *The Italian Job*. Not sure what Michael Caine would have thought of it but to the check-in girl's relief, Ed's case fell back and reversed back to check-in, along, of course, with several other cases that had been checked-in at different check-in desks. By now the boys behind Ed were getting desperate – some for the toilet, some for the bar, the nervous flyers amongst them just desperate.

"Could you open your suitcase and show me your passport sir?" said an increasingly frazzled check-in girl. Never one to understand the nuances of a woman's mind, Ed's attempt at levity fell way short of the mark. "Can't open it," he said. "I 'as locked the key in the suitcase."

If looks could kill, the check-in girl had just executed Ed in the most slow and painful way known to man! She'd seen the film and until now she knew the bloke on whom she was going to use the scalpel and forceps. This guy in front of her was rapidly rising to the top of her hit list.

"Only kidding. I am not that daft," said Ed and promptly opened his case to retrieve his passport which he had imaginatively packed amongst his new boxers. Sadly, and still smiling at the check-in girl, Ed failed to close his case before the 30 golf balls he had also packed, leapt out from his case and were now cascading to all parts of the airport check-in.

"You don't play golf Ed, why have you packed so many golf balls?"

"I live next to a golf course, see. My two boys' has been collecting balls for years. Nicking 'em, you might say." Ed's boys were in their mid 20s. "Thought I might give it a bash on holiday."

"What about clubs, Ed?"

Unfortunately, amidst the chaos, Ed's attempt at humour had been overheard by Hypo Harold who set off at a pace telling all and sundry that he had to sit down because his palpitations had started to kick in and that that silly bugger Ed had locked his passport in his suitcase and also locked his key in his suitcase.

"Why 'as he got your passport?" said Trev, only grasping part of the conversation.

Before Hypo could answer, Dai Bungalow not to be confused with Uncle Dai Bingo, had turned to Arwyn and asked, just loud enough for all to hear, "Why 'as Ed got Hypo Harold's keys and passport locked in 'is suitcase? I always thought Hypo was a bit, you know, odd like, and Ed's divorced now. Why is that, see? Perhaps that's why 'is missus ran off with the ugly bloke next door. Face like a slapped arse he has, and a hairy bugger too. It's like shakin' 'ands with a chimpanzee."

"When did you shake hands with a chimpanzee then, Dai?" came a call from the back of the queue... and by now the conversation was getting out of hand.

"I is not hypochondriac and Ed 'asn't got my key and passport," pleaded Harold, to no-one in particular.

Most of his golf balls retrieved, Ed meanwhile was skipping happily towards passport control and the departure lounge for that long awaited Tia Maria and Coke, one of the very few good things he could remember from his disastrous honeymoon. He had thought about asking for the check-in girl's telephone number, but decided he was old enough to be her father and he didn't want to embarrass her with all those people around. Besides, she seemed to have a lot on her plate and anyway, he knew where she worked.

Once they had resuscitated Hypo Harold, who had fainted

as news of his alleged relationship with the newly-divorced Ed had spread along the queue, the rest of the check-in passed with little or no incident. Amazingly Harold recovered 'sharpish like' the very instant Big Bri, the fireman, threatened to "insert my size twelve boot so far up your backside you'll be able to clean your teeth with my laces".

Arwyn reassured Harold that the boys were only joking. "Everyone knows Ed is a ladies' man and what with your health problems, Harold..."

Disappointed that he couldn't get a jug of sangria in the departure lounge, Ed had convinced the nervous Layton that Tia Maria and Coke was the ultimate Spanish drink. Layton ordered a large Tia Maria and Coke and another large Tia Maria and Coke. Most of the contents of Layton's stomach had been left by the bins at the club, while some remained on his, not so gleaming, new trainers. So, on an empty stomach, Layton had by now consumed several cans of Trev's cider, several of Hypo's travel pills and two large Tia Marias and Coke, the second of which saw Layton sprinting to the toilet where he threw up again and then fell asleep in a cubicle. Fortunately, the flight was delayed and, as the choir sang at the bar and made up for the missed visit to the pub, Layton slept and slowly sobered up. Unfortunately, sober and hung over is not the state the nervous Layton wanted to be as he was about to confront his fear of flying.

As the flight departure gate was announced Arwyn rallied the troops and only then realised that Layton was not in their midst. "You boys go on. We'll find him."

"I think he's still in the bog," said Ed, his own dickey stomach reminding him why he no longer drank Tia Maria and Coke.

"Come with me Bri," said Arwyn. "We'll get Layton." Layton was indeed still in the toilet but by now he was sober and frightened. It took all of Arwyn's reassurances and Bri's threats to get him to the departure gate. "Don't worry Layt, we're all in this together," Bill, the bus steward, ventured rather unhelpfully.

Determined not to let the side down, Layton bravely went to his seat. "It's probably not so bad after all," he thought as he clambered in to seat 24B, just before sweaty Trev clambered over him into window seat 24A and Hypo arrived to take aisle seat 24C. The whiff of Trev's armpit almost caused the third, or was it the fourth vomit of the day? However, a quick inhale/exhale into the bag, thoughtfully provided by the pretty trolley-dolly, calmed things down. Trapped, Layton felt it was so unfair that his final journey was to be taken sitting between Pavarotti's obese, smelly brother and Lily Savages hypochondriac old uncle. Or should that be aunt? Still the trolley-dolly was very pretty. Layton thought that perhaps the journey wouldn't be so bad after all.

Unfortunately, take-off and landing were nightmares for Layton and also for Trev and Harold. Shaking and sweating more profusely than even Trev on a summer's day, Layton insisted on holding their hands at take-off and on landing. The three of them shrieked as the deceptively strong Layton squeezed the life out of their fingers.

"I'll never play the piano again," said Harold as they collected their luggage.

"You never played it before," said Uncle Dai Bingo.

"Not the point," said Harold who promptly sought out the airport chemist and replenished his stock of travel sickness pills. He also bought some ointment for his battered and bruised fingers.

"Why does you want travel sickness pills now Harold? The hotel's not going nowhere," was one of the more pithy questions from someone in the tenor section.

The problem with a large group checking-in at a hotel is that someone will check-in first and someone has to be last.

"Oh, why is I always last?" said Harold as he asked the agreeable receptionist if she could find him a wheelchair.

"He doesn't need a wheelchair luv," said Bri. "My boot up his arse will get him up to his room if the lifts don't work."

Ed, meanwhile, was happy as a pig in the proverbial. He was first to get his key and his welcome glass of sangria reminded him of, apart from Tia Maria, the only good thing that came out of his last trip to Spain. Now on firm ground, Layton too had shed his inhibitions and was the first to discover that Spanish beer was cheaper than at home and not at all like the p**s he'd been told.

Everyone checked-in without too many problems. There was a yell and several expletives from Ed's room as he crashed into the coffee table.

"The lights don't work," he complained until his buttie told him, as politely as possible, exactly where he should insert his key card. "Let there be light... and there was light!"

In the morning, breakfast passed without too many mishaps. Without their wives along to remind them of the dangers of over eating and cholesterol, and not in the least put off by the sign which indicated the eggs were revolting (it should have read scrambled), the boys filled their boots. The 'late Gerald' lived up to his name by arriving for breakfast just as the waiting staff started clearing things away.

*

Dennis has two speeds... neither of which is particularly fast. As the choir's intrepid musical director, he had overseen many highs and the occasional low during his 20 years with the choir. Today Dennis had called a brief practice for 10 a.m. This was to be followed by a guided tour of the town that was to be their home for the next few days. To the amusement of the choir, Dennis turned up in a pair of baggy shorts several sizes too big for him. Each leg of Dennis' shorts resembled the wind sock that might have been used at Alicante airport and they ended just before his white socks and sandals began. Dennis' legs had not seen the sun in 30 years and they certainly were not going to see the sun in those shorts. Topped off by his ever present Dai cap and pipe, Dennis was the epitome of the Brit (of a certain age) abroad. The boys however, thought the world of Dennis and would follow him anywhere... usually out of a morbid curiosity.

Resplendent in his Man at C&A shorts and matching shirt, Ed strolled into practice only 30 minutes late. As he had forgotten to adjust his watch to Spanish time, he could have argued that he was 30 minutes early. Ed sported a new straw hat. He couldn't find a Kiss Me Kwik hat, so his refined taste drew him to the next tackiest. Somewhat incongruously, his hat bore the slogan 'I Luv Man U'.

"But you don't," said Arwyn.

"Don't what?" said Ed.

"Love Manchester United."

"Suppose not," said Ed, "but someone has to." Appropriately, given his new sartorial elegance, Ed was carrying a copy of the *Sun* newspaper.

"Walked bloody miles for this. Cost a fortune and I read it at the airport yesterday."

"That's because it is yesterday's paper. They are a day late out here," explained Arwyn. These were the days before English newspapers were printed in Madrid and distributed on the Costas.

Dennis was happy with the meeting and the brief practice and so it was a happy group that met their guides. The bus took them around and they stopped at the various points of interest. A Valleys choir, not all the boys appreciated the humour when their Welsh guide pointed out that the sea was on their left and that even though they were from the Valleys, they should easily recognise it as it could be found between the sand and the sky! The guide even took the choir to a typical Spanish tapas bar and, apart from Trev complaining about the size of the portions, everyone enjoyed the experience. Given that he'd eaten enough at breakfast to feed a small school, even Trev didn't really mind about the size of the portions. A bodega was visited and the boys were suitably amused when the handwritten sign on the large wooden doors was translated for them, 'Sangria, antidepressivo sangria aqui' (Here Sangria, antidepressant sangria).

"Antidepressant sangria? Not sure about that," said Hypo Harold. "I am always as miserable as sin after sangria!"

"You are always as miserable as sin," came a chorus of replies.

The only incident, if it could be called an incident, happened when the guide mentioned that the old church, where they were due to sing that evening, was the oldest building in the town and the only building to survive the earthquake of 1820. To almost everyone's amusement, Arwyn asked if 1820 meant 20 past six (as in 18:20) and, as he did so, Hypo Harold, who hadn't really been listening, on hearing the word earthquake, started to rummage around in his bag for valium.

"Did he say an earthquake at 20 past six tonight?"

Not for the last time on the trip, Harold believed the earth was moving and for all the wrong reasons. He convinced himself that the rumbling noises were something far more sinister than Trev's stomach, and he almost fainted again when the mayor set off the fireworks that were prepared especially to welcome the choir to his town. A couple of large Spanish brandy's compensated somewhat for the lack of valium.

"But Dennis don't like the boys drinking before a concert," said Harold as Dennis handed him another brandy!

El Concierto – The Concert

A much understated part of choir life is the amount of money choirs raise for charity. Most of our choirs are amateur choirs. They pay for their own trips, costs which are only sometimes supplemented by fundraising. The choristers are in it for the love of singing and for the camaraderie of being with their friends. Wherever they go, choirs raise huge amounts of money for local charities.

I have yet to work with a choir that didn't actively raise funds for deserving causes. At home our choirs happily support local and national charities, not only performing free of charge on a regular basis, but the choristers often contribute from their own pockets. Many choirs also adopt a charity and fundraise for the charity throughout the course of a year, or even over many years.

Whilst on tour, our groups are invariably happy to perform in support of whatever deserving cause is relevant to the location. When organising a concert this wonderful mind-set serves several purposes. Of course, the main purpose of any event of this type is to raise money for the charity concerned, but to do so, people have to turn up and support the event. It is very disappointing for the choir if, having travelled so far, nobody turns up to their concert. Involving a charity can certainly help attract an audience and if the choir perform well, as they invariably do, the audience is happy, the choir is happy, the charity is happy and much needed funds are raised to boost the charity coffers.

Our touring choirs have raised funds for a wide range of charities, but this concert was in aid of *Asociacion Espanola Contra El Cancer* – a Spanish and ex-pat charity that specialise in prevention, screening and helping those unfortunate enough to have that dreadful disease. Many volunteers donate a considerable amount of their time, and expertise, to help charities function, and this particular branch of AECC was a great example of the local Spanish people working hand in hand with their new friends from the UK who have chosen to live in their town.

The concert was to take place immediately after Mass in the main church in town. The plan was for the choir to line up outside the church and then, almost as soon as Mass had ended, they were to march to the altar singing 'Sanctus'. For his part the priest, before disappearing for a cigarette and a brandy, would remind the congregation that a concert was about to begin and those who wanted to stay were welcome to do so. Some of the congregation, of course, would leave but these were soon replaced by those who had been eagerly and patiently waiting outside the church. The concert was free to all, so in order to raise funds, the charity had permission to set up their stall outside the church where they rattled their tins and sold raffle tickets, tombola and assorted gifts which had been donated by a generous public.

The choir scrubbed up remarkably well and now, suited and booted, the boys congregated in the hotel reception, patiently awaiting their bus. One or two, well perhaps four or five, had gone to the bar, but no serious amount of alcohol was being consumed. They had been warned by Arwyn, and Dennis' gentle pep talk had reminded the boys of their responsibilities, to themselves, to the charity, to the audience, to their village and most of all, to the choir.

"Your chariot awaits," announced the guide on arrival of the bus and one by one the boys filed on to the coach. Some, of course, hung around until bus steward Bill yelled, "Get on the bus. I 'as to count you buggers on. Don't want to leave anyone behind."

One short. "Where is Gerald? Is he late again?"

An irate Arwyn jumped off the bus via the front door to find the 'late Gerald'. At exactly that moment the, by now, 'ten minutes late Gerald', leapt on the bus via the back door.

"'Ow is you always late, butt?" asked a flustered Bill. "It's a talent, I suppose," said Gerald, to no-one in particular.

"Someone go and find Arwyn," said Bill.

At last the bus pulled away from the hotel. Although only ten minutes to the venue, the streets were narrow and, at that time of the evening, quite busy. At least it gave the guides time to introduce the drivers. "Your driver tonight is Adolfo." Polite applause for Adolfo. "Tomorrow your driver will be

Attila. That's right, those amongst you who are listening and have at least a grasp of the Spanish language, will realise you are being driven this week, by Adolf and Attila! You couldn't make it up, could you?"

As Adolfo expertly negotiated the narrow streets, Hypo Harold was searching for his pills. His natural nervousness before a concert, combined with the thought of being driven to a town on an earthquake belt by a madman called Adolf, was sure to set off his ulcer. Harold's demeanour wasn't helped when the guide announced that the bus company was so pleased with Adolfo they were even considering paying for him to take his driving test next week!

The boys were impressed by the atmosphere in the streets around the church and especially in the square. Just as there is something special about a floodlit sports fixture, the street lighting and the hundreds of people milling around the square, in the cafés and bars, added to the electricity in the air. The choir made its way through the crowded square stopping only to offer the assembled throng a burst of the Welsh national anthem. "Not sure it would be appropriate in the church," confided Dennis. "Attracted a bit of attention, mind. Can't but help with the audience."

And so it proved. By now the square was packed and our heroes were soon surrounded by curious local children and what seemed like hundreds of ex-pat Welsh who had come to see the choir. They all joined in with the anthem. Plenty of other British ex-pats were about and all things pointed to a packed and cosmopolitan audience. The church held over 1,000 so this was a result. Unfortunately the priest taking Mass was not the usual guy. He was on holiday and the replacement for the night seemed determined to wring every last second out of his moment in the limelight, so he went on and on and on.

"The boys are ready. When do we go on, then?" asked Dai Bungalow.

"It's his 'ouse" said Dennis. "I don't suppose we can physically remove him. Be patient."

"It's not fair, mun," said, of all people, the late Gerald. "We is already 15 minutes late."

"That's rich coming from you," said Arwyn, accompanied by several choristers telling Gerald exactly where he could stick his opinion on timekeeping!

"OK boys, he's just about finished," said Hypo Harold, who understood the workings of a Catholic Mass. With a definite lack of sensitivity about the church, Dai Bungalow chimed in with, "I do 'ope the priest 'as nailed their feet to the floor or they will all bugger off when they know it is us they 'as to listen to."

The choir lined up and marched in, two columns down either aisle, to 'Sanctus'. A packed church, extra chairs hastily borrowed from the local bars, was crackling with a unique and indescribable mixture of excitement and respect.

An hour later the boys emerged from the church, beaming smiles giving away their feelings on a memorable, never to be forgotten concert. Thirty minutes later they managed to get away from the hundreds of Spanish and ex-pats who wanted to congratulate them or merely speak with someone from home.

"I was crying when you sang 'Gwahoddiad'," recounted an elderly mother with her middle-aged daughter. "Was we that bad, then," asked Ed, who, thoroughly enjoying himself and taking advantage of his new-found celebrity status, now had his eyes on the middle-aged daughter. Much to the annoyance of the put-upon waiters, but to the delight of the bar owner, the boys seemed to have picked up dozens of groupies on their way to the bar which was now home for the after concert celebrations.

Jugs of beer and sangria flowed freely and Ed ordered a round of Tia Marias for his mates who now included an elderly mother and her middle-aged daughter. Of course, with free beer to be drunk, his mates ignored the Tia Maria. Ed was not ignoring Tia Maria. Indeed Ed and Layton were getting on famously with Mary and Kathy. Mary, it seems, was not Kathy's mother. She was her auntie.

"Auntie Mary, that's Tia Maria in Spanish," said young Layton, just out of college. "It's a sign Ed. You are in here, and Auntie Mary seems a laugh but she's not really my type, ta-ra."

Spotting his chance of a seat and with his eye crucially on the remnants of the food, Trev jumped into Layton's chair. Trev and his odours were not high on Ed's list of companions when planning a romantic evening, but Ed spotted his chance. Trev's arrival on the scene, and the stunned look of dismay on Kathy's face offered him the opportunity to invite the ever more fanciable Kathy out on to the terrace. To be fair, recently wounded by divorce, Ed wanted nothing more than some pleasant female company. Rather than sit opposite Trev, who by now seemed to have something from the buffet crawling into, or out of his mouth, Kathy accepted Ed's invitation to the terrace. Ever the gentleman, Ed reached across the table to kiss the hand of Auntie Mary. Unfortunately the mixture of sangria, beer and everyone's Tia Maria, had blurred his vision and undermined his balance. On grasping Auntie Mary's hand and bowing over the table to kiss it, Ed managed to burn the back of Mary's hand on the candle. Mary shrieked with pain and knocked the remaining Tia Maria and half a jug of sangria over Ed's pale grey choir slacks.

"Lovin' F***," screamed Ed as the other candle arrowed its way towards his groin.

"Phew, that was lucky," exclaimed Trev, as he cradled the remaining plate of food.

"Good job she 'ad the good sense to throw the sangria over you Ed. Imagine what damage that candle would 'ave done to your todger if it 'ad hit!" said Big Bri, desperately trying, and failing, to stifle a laugh! Any pretence at romance had gone

27

out of the window as Ed surveyed the damage in the typically small and overcrowded toilet.

"'Ow is I going to pull now? Look at the mess on my trousers," moaned Ed.

"Never mind Ed, there's plenty more sangria where that came from and you can borrow some slacks from Hypo for the concert. He's about your size," Arwyn chuckled.

Never one to dwell on events, Ed returned to the scene of his latest faux pas. Kathy and Mary were nowhere to be seen and the boys had started singing in the other room. Between mouthfuls of rice, Trev mumbled, "they've gone".

"Why? Wot you say to them?" Ed enquired innocently.

The morning after the night before

The next day was free for the choir and most of them needed it. However, Arwyn and Dennis were a little concerned about leaving the boys to their own devices for too long.

"What shall we do then, Den?" asked one of the Dais as Dennis surveyed the motley assortment of Speedos, shorts, bathers, and rolled-up trousers that had outdone the Germans and grabbed all the sun beds around the pool.

"Ain't no Germans 'ere, butt," said Uncle Dai, "they is all in Majorca."

Until that moment, Arthur, the bald village barber, had been noticeable by his absence and, carrying the scars of the previous evening, he now made his first appearance of the day.

"Arthur, wot's that on your head?" Dennis almost asked. He was stopped mid question by a swift dig in the ribs from Big Bri.

"Shh, 'e 'asn't noticed yet and I don't want to be around when he does!"

"Missed breakfast I suppose?" asked Arthur, more in hope than expectation. "And why is everyone giggling when I walks past?"

"Ask the guy behind the bar if you is 'ungry, he'll do you one of 'em Spanish omelette thingys – Tortugas." Tortuga is the Spanish word for tortoise.

"You mean tortilla," said Layton, just out of college, "and what's that on your head?"

"What do you mean, what's on my head? There is nothing on my head," said Arthur, as he somehow tried to look at the top of his pate. Big Bri exited swiftly!

What was on Arthur's head?

After the previous evening's concert and having partaken of a few free beers, Arthur, Big Bri and Justin and one or two others, had gone off in search of a stronger drink. Several vodkas later, Arthur wandered back to the choir party and, just as Mary and Kathy were leaving, sat at a table where he promptly fell asleep. Ten minutes later, and concerned that their mate was still asleep, Bri and the boys did what any friend would do in similar circumstances. They shot off to the nearby street market and purchased some children's crayons!

Blissfully unaware of the Salvador Dali-esque happy smiling face that had been drawn on the canvas that was his large and completely bald head, Arthur awoke with a start and joined the choir in their afterglow pub repertoire. The last thing he could remember from the night before was Adolfo pointing to his head and saying something in Spanish, before giggling to himself and bidding Arthur farewell!

"See you Mañana – tomorrow, señor smiley face."

"Smiley face? I'm sure he just said 'smiley face'." Arthur was bewildered – tired and happy, but bewildered. And so he had gone to bed.

Ed and the boys returned from the beach where they'd gone for a stroll. Ed was carrying yet another copy of the *Sun* newspaper, the same edition he had bought on each of the previous two days. This time he blamed the Stevie Wonder-style sunglasses he'd bought from the ever so friendly 'looky

looky' man. As he crashed into the not so automatic door, Ed realised these amazing sunglasses did not work so well indoors. "Can't see a thing in these glasses. Hi Arthur butt, wot is that on your 'ed?" said Ed.

"Where can we see the flamingo dancers?" asked Dai Bungalow. At this point Dennis decided that perhaps leaving the boys to their own devices was probably the best option. He felt a bit queasy.

"Must be something I've eaten," he said as he retired to his room balcony with his book, cap and pipe.

Most of the boys spent the afternoon sleeping by the pool. Most remembered sunblock. Ed, of course didn't. Not only did he not remember sun-cream, he also fell asleep wearing his sunglasses and his C&A vest. It was a good job that Ed, despite his Man U hat, actually supported Arsenal, because when he woke up his red and white torso resembled an Arsenal shirt in reverse. White body, red shoulders and arms, while the large white circles around his eyes reminded everyone of the long-extinct red panda. It hadn't really been Ed's day. He was quite a sight at the bar. What a dilemma. Should he keep his huge sunglasses on at night and look a proper tit, and a proper tit with severely restricted vision, or should he remove them and look a proper tit but at least be able to see who was laughing at him?

Andrew, a large bass baritone, hadn't spent his afternoon by the pool. Instead he and a few intrepid mates had decided to visit the nearby stretch of sandy beach. Sitting with his mates at a beach bar, Andrew had an ulterior motive for wanting to be on the beach. On a morning stroll he had noticed the tiny Oriental girls who were strolling up and down the beach offering massage to the sun worshippers. Genuine massage, therapeutic, nothing dodgy. The type of head and foot massage guaranteed to alleviate stress, ease the stiff neck, and get rid of backache. After 20 years packing down in the front row of the scrum and being an enlightened soul, Andrew occasionally visited a chiropractor at home. With his resolve strengthened by a few strong Spanish beers in the sunshine, he moved on to the beach and called over one of the tiny Asian girls. He genuinely hoped that she might ease some of the stiffness and ache in his back and shoulders that had built up on the journey to Spain. His discomfort had been exacerbated by a few nights trying to sleep in a bed that was obviously not designed for an ex-prop forward who weighed in at 19 stone plus. Besides, if all else failed, was there a better way to while away 45 minutes or so, than to be gently massaged by a delightful Asian girl whilst sitting under a palm tree?

The tiny girl laid her mat on the sand and Andrew sat in the appropriate position. When sitting upright, Andrew was almost the same height as his tiny masseuse when she stood behind him. His mates, fuelled by the strong Spanish beer, looked on with a mixture of curiosity and bawdy humour. The girl started her massage and suddenly all seemed well in Andrew's world. He loved his wife dearly but now he was away with his mates in the choir, sitting in the sunshine, enjoying a few beers and a gentle massage from a beautiful girl. His back was sure to improve.

Unfortunately, after a few minutes or so it soon became obvious to the tiny masseuse that all was not well in her world. As a prop forward of 20 years standing, or should that be crouching? – Andrew had developed incredibly strong shoulders and neck muscles and whatever the tiny masseuse tried, the tiny masseuse wasn't going to release the tension in those shoulders. Not on the beach, in 45 minutes. At this point Andrew didn't particularly care. His concert tour was over; a sore throat not cured by any of Hypo Harold's pills was likely to prevent him singing tomorrow. As he dozed Andrew was probably dreaming of a few cold beers before he returned to the hotel to shower before the evening's festivities.

Andrew's dreams were about to turn into a nightmare.

Unable to release the tension in those massive shoulders and keen for Andrew to get his money's worth, the tiny masseuse called for reinforcements which arrived in the shape of her formidable looking older brother. Andrew's mates looked on as the tiny masseuse's brother approached. He was built like the Incredible Hulk after he'd been riled, mixed with the demeanour of Genghis Khan. Much to the amusement of Andrew's mates, who of course offered no warning to their buttie, Genghis set about Andrew's shoulders with the vigour of a cage fighter, or perhaps a Samoan rugby flanker.

Andrew woke with a start. No longer dreaming of his tiny masseuse, all thoughts of his next pint had even vanished, as Andrew sensed he was being mugged... but on the beach... and where were his mates, his butties... where was the cavalry riding to his rescue? Just in time, Andrew spotted his mates as they fell about laughing. Big Bri even spilt his beer, an act for which he incurred a fine from the committee. Fortunately Andrew spotted his mates a split-second before he delivered his retaliatory punch on Genghis. Unfortunately, a split-second after the tiny masseuse, fearing for her brother's safety (Ho! Ho!) had delivered an expert karate kick to the back of Andrew's legs which saw him tumble into the sand. Fortunately, an international incident was avoided before Big Bri piled in. To his eternal credit, Andrew apologised to Genghis and sister for the misunderstanding and, after a beer to calm the nerves and a Coke each for his massage team, and a dip in the sea to remove the sand that had clung to the oils on his body when he tumbled into the sand, the massage continued. Who knows, addresses may even have been exchanged?

"She'd obviously had a night out in Merthyr," Andrew opined later as he ruefully felt his calves.

Afterwards, at the quiz night, Andrew swore that it was the best massage he'd ever had.

"This is the best I've felt in years," said Andrew. "Whose

round is it? I'll have another pint please. Could someone pass it over? I think I've done something to my shoulder? Can you pass a straw?"

Quiz Night

After the exertions of the past couple of days, the choir decided it would be a good idea to hold their monthly quiz night.

"It'll keep the boys out of the bar for an hour," said Bill.

So at 21.00 hours, the boys congregated in the bar for the quiz.

Back home they ran a monthly quiz at the Welfare, £1 each to enter, £10 first prize with all the proceeds going towards choir funds. This amounted to a useful fundraiser as everyone was expected to pay their pound, whether or not they chose to enter the quiz. This quiz was to be 2 Euros each to enter with 10 Euros as first prize and the rest of the money would go towards tomorrow night's farewell drink.

"We 'as a bit of a slush fund," said Bill.

I sometimes wonder if every choir, social group, sports team has a member or members who devote large chunks of their lives compiling or competing in quizzes? The choir quiz compilers were retired teachers, Dafydd Jones, known as Dic and Paul Jones known as Gazza.

"Lots of brains those two," said old Tom. Tom, the eldest member of the touring party had regaled everyone for years with his tales of running off to fight in the Spanish Civil War. Were this true, Tom must have been well over 90 years of age, a fact not necessarily borne out by his passport. He had probably read Laurie Lee's *As I Walked Out One Midsummer Morning* and perhaps he'd even read some Lorca. No doubt he had been to Spain before, but unless he ran away aged ten, it was unlikely he had fought in the Spanish Civil War. He might just have made World War II and certainly Suez, but not the Spanish Civil War.

"Lots of brains," repeated Tom, "but not an ounce of common sense between them. Teachers see. Never left school. Man and boy, 40 years in school. Plenty of brains but nobody ever awarded a degree for common sense to a teacher, did they? A degree of common sense would be a bonus with those two."

"Get us a whisky bach," Old Tom asked Arwyn, blaming his war wound for not going to the bar himself. "Intelligence is knowing a tomato is a fruit, wisdom is knowing not to put one in your fruit salad," said Tom to no-one in particular. "No common sense, teachers. Never left school. Cheers butt, thanks for the whisky, diolch."

Layton, the youngest and newest member of the choir asked his Uncle Dai why the boys' nicknames were Dic when his name was Dafydd Jones and Gazza when his name was Paul Jones? The name Gazza seemed a particularly incongruous name for a quizmaster.

"Well," explained Uncle Dai, "Dic is short for dictionary. He knows lots of big words but we can't call 'im 'Dictionary' so Dic, it is. Gazza? Well it's obvious really. His name is Paul, but 'cos 'e is always doin' quizzes and suchlike, we calls 'im Bamber after Bamber Gascoigne. You know 'im that used to do *University Challenge*. Gascoigne = Gazza. Obvious really. We was goin' to call 'im Cy, as in enCYclopedia but that's too confusing."

As Layton pondered this simple logic, the Jones boys, Dic and Gazza, drew lots to see who partnered who in the two-man quiz teams.

"Doesn't that 'stuffing' bloke do *University Challenge?*" asked Dai Bungalow. "You know's, that Jeremy Paxo?"

"First team out of the hat – Andrew and Ed," announced Dic Dictionary.

After their respective afternoons on the beach and by the pool, Andrew and Ed made for an interesting combination. By now Andrew had stiffened up and was supping his beer through a straw. He struggled to the Gents and, on his return, found his pint and straw had been joined by a cocktail umbrella and sparklers. Ed looked very, er, dapper. Having discarded his 'Stevie Wonders', he obviously preferred to see who was laughing at him. He had chosen to wear his spanking new luminous white C&A shirt to show off his tan. His panda eyes, set off by his luminous shirt, shone out from his now ruddy red face.

"Trev" (who had ordered a plate of chips to ward off his hunger pangs), "will team up with Dai Bungalow," announced Gazza. Both Trev and Dai thought they'd drawn the booby prize.

"That's a marriage made in heaven" said Arwyn. "Ignorance and Chips."

It seems that Edwina Currie allegedly once announced to anyone daft enough to listen to her, that northerners were likely to live shorter lives than their southern counterparts because of 'ignorance and chips'.

"Must have been talking about Dai Bungalow and Trev," thought Arwyn.

Young Layton, "just out of college see" and Hypo Harold were installed as favourites.

"Should 'ave all the medical and pop questions covered," reasoned Arthur, who had been drawn with his good mate and roommate Justin, a youngish, 30-something tenor. Unfortunately, in his room's mirrored bathroom, Arthur had eventually seen the smiley face drawn on the back of his head. Fortunately he had managed to wash his head clean. Unfortunately he had blamed Justin and Big Bri for the prank and had sworn revenge. Once again Big Bri had managed to exit stage left, leaving Justin to his fate.

So that we don't lose the will to live, I'll skip the quiz, except to mention a small selection of the questions, plus some unlikely answers.

Quizmaster Gazza: "Topical question boys. *Erythema*

Solaris is the medical term for what common ailment? It's particularly prevalent amongst daft choristers who fall asleep by the pool. Are you listening ED?"

Answer: Sunburn.

Ed actually got this wrong. He thought the answer was snoring.

Quizmaster Dic: "Not another dig at Ed, but which rays produce sunburn?"

Answer: Ultraviolet.

"Did I tell you I was in the Spanish Civil War?" said Old Tom. "Well I fought alongside a big Spanish bird called Ultra Violet. Hell of a girl, Violet. She used to flash 'er Bristols at the enemy. Sniper shot 'er straight between the eyes. Thought I was in there," Tom mused sadly, to no-one in particular. "Are you goin' to the bar, Bill? Get me a whisky. Cheers, butt."

Quizmaster Dic: "Who wrote *Portnoys Complaint?*"

"Portnoys? Is that one of Hypo's complaints?" Arwyn asked.

"I is not a hypochondriac," shouted Harold and stomped his foot for effect! "Ooh, I think I've twisted my ankle," Harold whispered to his teammate, Layton.

Answer: Philip Roth

Quizmaster Gazza: "One for bookie Steve – which American actor / comedian said, 'Horse sense is the thing a horse has that stops it betting on men'?"

Answer: W.C. Fields.

Quizmaster Gazza: "Who wrote 40 whingers on a bus?"

"Never 'eard of that," was the general consensus.

"Just a joke. Actually it was Mike, our bus driver. Sent Arwyn a message this afternoon. The message said, 'How are the whingers doing?'

Quizmaster Dic: "What was the name of Rigsby's cat in the TV series *Rising Damp?*"

Pussy, Cat, Tiger, Paris and somewhat imaginatively, Strudel, were amongst the answers.

Answer: Vienna.

"Don't I get a point for strudel?" asked food correspondent Trev. "I knew it was something Austrian."

"Interesting concept," said one of the Jones boys, "but is strudel Austrian?"

"If that's the case, I should get a point for Paris," said Justin. "I knew it was an European capital city."

"What's *Rising Damp* anyway and who is Rigsby?" asked young Layton? Just out of college, see.

Remarkably, after almost an hour being grilled by the sadistic quizmasters, we had a tie! We are not going to say which team finished last. Suffice to say Dai Bungalow blamed Trev for buggering off for 20 minutes to buy a burger.

"OK, tie-break question. First to raise his hand. Name a commonly used six-letter word that contains no 'true' vowels?"

After a few minutes silence, quizmaster Dic said, "A bit of a clue. Very few of you buggers 'as this."

Layton's hand shoots up. "Rhythm" he announces triumphantly, "and rhythms is a seven-letter word."

"Clever bugger – just left college see," said Uncle Dai Bingo.

"Correct," said quizmaster Gazza "and we would have accepted 'sylphs'. 'Sylphs', we thought Athletic Trev might 'ave got that."

Trev was too engrossed with the gherkin in his burger to come up with a witty response.

"I knew the answer," said Andrew "but I couldn't raise my arm quick enough!"

The night passed relatively quietly except, perhaps, in Justin and Arthur's room. Having each drunk a little too much, Justin was becoming maudlin and was bemoaning the fact that he had never had a serious girlfriend. As a 30-something ginger with thinning locks and ginger beard, he felt there was no hope of this being rectified anytime soon. Living with Mam probably didn't help.

Arthur was not beyond a practical joke himself. Oblivious to the consequences and sensing the opportunity for a little light hearted revenge for the smiley face episode, Bald Barber Arthur set about convincing Justin that he would have more chance with the ladies if he did something to his hair and shaved off his beard.

"I will do your 'air when we gets back – pop in the shop next week. We'll do your beard now."

And so it was that professional, but drunk, Bald Barber Arthur set about shaving off Justin's ginger beard – "no charge, mind".

Justin's usual skin tone could generally be best described as milk bottle white but, after a few days in the Spanish sun, despite factor 56, Justin's face and head were now a similar colour to the shirt of his beloved Scarlets. 'The Only Scarlet Supporter in the Choir' might have been a forerunner to *Little Britain*'s 'Only Gay in the Village'. Well, most of Justin's face was bright red. The portion of his face previously covered by a five year old growth of, admittedly trimmed, beard still retained its milk bottle white hue.

Despite, or perhaps because of, his alcohol intake, Arthur immediately regretted shaving Justin's beard. This deep regret was heightened when Justin said how he had tried to convince Big Bri not to draw the smiley face on Arthur's head.

"Was funny though," said Justin, as he rubbed his new smooth and very white chin.

Arthur's feeling of deep remorse was further heightened the following morning when he was woken by a scream from the bathroom. "What 'ave you done to me," screamed Justin on entering the mirrored bathroom for his morning ablutions. "I'm all blotches, like!" Arthur felt terrible... and his hangover hadn't kicked in yet!

Concierto numero dos

It was an interesting looking male voice choir that lined up for their choir photo on the steps of the town's 600-capacity theatre, the venue for that night's concert. As is normal in Spain, the audience mingle in the bars and squares around the concert venues. Cameras flashed as the choir lined up for its photo shoot.

Ed couldn't remove the sangria stains from his trousers, so had to wear a different colour pair of slacks from the rest of the choir and was relegated to the middle of the back row for the photo shoot. If anything, his skin tone had darkened and the white panda eyes stood out in the lights. Ed had also been fined for wearing the wrong trousers. Standing next to Ed was the newly clean-shaven Justin, he of the red and white face.

"Oi Justin. You as forgotten your beard," shouted Dai Bungalow. "Shall we go back for it?"

Andrew, who earlier in the day had completely stiffened up, had managed to get himself off the sofa and to the bus. He was walking a bit like Boris Karloff did as Frankenstein. A couple of the boys borrowed a trolley from a Spanish lorry driver who was delivering crates to a local bar. They hoped they could wheel Andrew to the concert… but Andrew was 19 stone…

The proceeds from the concert were to be shared between the aforementioned AECC and the town's Alzheimer Association, another joint Spanish / ex-pat charity that does wonderful work for those unfortunates who suffer from this debilitating illness and the families who care for their loved ones.

Of course, the concert was a resounding success and, as always, the choir rose to the occasion and entertained a capacity audience for almost two hours.

Dennis particularly wanted to thank Justin who, as one of the soloists, played a major role in the proceedings. "You sang well tonight Justin. You should shave your beard off more often!"

In the euphoria following the successful concert, Justin had almost forgotten.

Homeward bound

Age and alcohol had at last caught up with some of the boys. They had to get up in the morning and, sensibly for once, the post concert afterglow singsong was a fairly low-key affair.

Big Bri had found a dartboard and, knowing he had a 'ringer' in the choir, he challenged the locals and the ex-pats to a darts' challenge.

Unfortunately, Andrew, who could barely lift his arm to his shoulder, was his 'ringer'. Andrew had played darts to a good standard as a young man, and still occasionally represented the local pub league select team. As a much younger man he had beaten "you knows who 'e beat – that 'crusty Cockney' bloke. You knows 'is name," said Dai Bungalow.

"Jocky Wilson," said Arwyn.

"No, I means that crusty Cockney – Jocky Wilson was Scottish – crusty Cockney was from, well Cockney land. Essex, is it?"

"No, I knows he was from somewhere in London."

"I know Jocky Wilson was Scottish," said an ever more exasperated Arwyn, "but it was Jocky Wilson who Andrew did beat when he was on an exhibition tour when he came to the Valleys. Andrew took a set off 'im. He never beat Eric Bristow – the *crafty* Cockney."

"Might 'ave done, if Eric 'ad ever come to the Valleys," said Dai Bungalow, "and who was the Welsh bloke? Big bugger."

Still slurping his beer through a straw, Andrew was certainly not fit for the darts challenge and so the choir darts' team slumped to an inglorious defeat. Unfortunately, the Euros raised by the quiz night also disappeared as Big Bri had bet the money on Andrew. Charitably, the victorious ex-pats donated their winnings to the charity, which is exactly what the choir had intended to do!

Straight after breakfast the following morning, Adolfo collected the boys, the 'late Gerald' carrying his breakfast in a napkin. Bill counted everybody onto the bus and with a wave and a song for the reception staff, it was off to the airport.

As on the outbound plane journey, Hypo Harold and Trev were due to sit with Layton. However, this time they had forced him into the window seat and Trev grasped Layton's hand. They couldn't afford any more bruised fingers. Layton slept through the entire journey. Well almost through the entire journey. Sitting behind, Dai Bungalow, tapped Layton on the head, "Wake up Layton, we is about to land. Look at the view."

The trip took place before the more relaxed, some might say more enlightened, rules about duty free tax paid goods came into force. In those days there was a strict limit to the amount of drinks, cigarettes and tobacco that one could bring into the country. During their stay in Spain, a few of the boys had stocked up on their duty free allocation. Was it for personal use only? A few extra bottles of brandy couldn't hurt, plus a few thousand cigs each for Mr Singh to sell at the corner shop.

"They never check at the airport," said one of the Dais.

Despite his ruined trousers Ed was happy. He'd had a wonderful time and, as ever, was eager to help. So, the boys placed all their cases onto Ed's trolley.

"They'd never stop Ed – he's an innocent abroad," said Big Bri.

Ed had enjoyed a wonderful break with the choir and was a happy soul. As they proceeded through customs, the lady in front of Ed was called over by an attractive female customs official to have her bags searched. Ed liked women in uniform and so, to everyone's horror, Ed joined the queue.

CHAPTER 2

Alfonso's Tale

IT WAS AGREED that the best way to finish the concert of the two choirs, one from Wales, the other from Spain, would be for them to sing the last item together. The Torrevieja concert would end with the rousing 'Chorus of the Hebrew Slaves' from Verdi's *Nabucco*.

Everyone was happy with this agreement. Everyone that is, except the two sets of choristers. Each group knew the music, but not the words in a mutual language and there was definitely no time for a rehearsal. So, before an audience of 2,000 people and after a brief break for the Spanish singers to grab a cigarette and a nip from their flasks, the Welsh and Spanish male voice choirs joined forces. Completely unrehearsed, they performed the famous piece, with the Welsh, in black suits, singing it in English, and the Spanish, also in black suits, singing it in Italian. The audience loved it and everyone who witnessed the exciting, impromptu finalé, still have fond memories of the occasion.

Everyone that is, except Alfonso.

Alfonso had recently moved to Torrevieja, and immediately joined a choir. After proving his ability as a singer, he was presented with his black choir blazer. Pleased to have already made friends in his new town, Alfonso set off on a well-deserved holiday. Ringing in his ears were the instructions that he return for what was to be his first concert with his new choir. True to his word, Alfonso arrived in his new town in time for his big night.

Being unfamiliar with his new area and not blessed with particularly good eyesight, Alfonso was unsure of how to find the venue. Rather than perched on his nose, his glasses were inside the pocket of his new and ill-fitting choir suit jacket. Just as he thought about retrieving them, he caught sight of several men, also kitted out in black jackets, stubbing out their cigarettes. Alfonso followed them into the auditorium and onto the stage where he forced his way into line, and stood exactly where his musical director had told him at the very first rehearsal. The Welsh choir sang in English and the Spanish choir in Italian... and Alfonso? Well he had never heard this music or the languages in which it was being sung. He looked to his left, then to his right, and when he eventually rescued his glasses, from deep inside his ill-fitting jacket, he focused hard on the female conductor. He looked at her through his jam jar lenses. Female conductor? The Russian conductor of his new choir was definitely a man. Where was the hirsute Gregory? The choir was now being conducted by a woman. What kind of madness was this?

Totally unaware of what was going on, but very aware that he was in the wrong place, all he could do was cringe. Alfonso was trapped. He could hardly march off the stage. The Welsh choir thought he was part of the Spanish choir. The Spanish guys thought he belonged to Wales. They were each too polite to ask the other. Under normal circumstances Alfonso would have slipped away and no-one would have uncovered his monumental mistake. Unfortunately there was little chance of a discreet escape. The concert was being recorded for local television. There was no hiding place. Indeed, on the television recording, the directors edited highlights seemed to focus on poor Alfonso's confusion. Life can be cruel.

And what of the original concert that had persuaded Alfonso to cut short his holiday? The concert in which he should have been singing, the concert in which he thought he was singing, had been cancelled because it seems a Welsh choir were arriving in town and were to give a concert with another town choir. Being a new boy on the block, nobody at his new choir had thought to contact him. Everyone had left it to someone else to tell Alfonso about the change of plan.

Complete with a new and improved pair of glasses, Alfonso, somewhat disillusioned with his choir soon joined another. To this day the boys still rib him about his first 'performance' with them and their friends from Wales.

Sometimes in Wales, I play and replay that part of the DVD of the concert recording. As I write this I can picture Alfonso's face, startled as if caught in the glare of the headlights of 4,000 eyes. It is amusing to see Alfonso look around him, to his left and to his right then behind him, knocking choristers on either side only to be pushed back into some sort of straight line.

CHAPTER 3

Is Wales in Africa?

ALFONSO'S STORY REMINDS me of the many, mostly amusing, incidents and events that have happened during the 20 years or so I have organized trips for choirs. Inevitably many of the stories seem to involve food and drink.

Did you know that supermarkets in university towns and cities throughout Britain are on a special alert at the start of a new term? Managers are told to stock up with millions of tubs of Pot Noodles, the staple diet for a large number of students. Similarly, the management at one hotel our Welsh choirs sometimes visit on the Costa Blanca, were ready for the onslaught of the choristers. Continental breakfasts were put on the back burner, in a manner of speaking, and the hotel regularly sent out to the British supermarkets for oceans of baked beans and vast supplies of bacon and sausage – the Spanish have their own eggs!

It is fascinating to observe the Brits at breakfast time. As a nation we are renowned for the way we spend an inordinate amount of time queuing. Choristers are no exception. Unlike some nationalities it never dawns on us that it might be more sensible to sit and wait till the crowds at the buffet thin out (as opposed to 'fat out'). The danger with this course of action, or inaction, is that the greedy buggers in the tenor section will have scoffed the lot by the time you get to the buffet. Perhaps we are just eager to dive into the mountain of food waiting to greet us so that we can get on with the rest of our day. Or maybe we are secretly hoping that those in front will abandon the idea of waiting and return to their seats. Fat chance, but who knows?

At this particular hotel, although the restaurant had waiters, the buffet was self-service. One just lifted up the tureen lids and it was every man for himself. Some headed for their table with the satisfied smile of a job well done. Their plates bulge with a mound of food as high as Snowdon. Others are going for three peaks, with additional helpings for Helvellyn and Ben Nevis.

The food was sometimes not seen as supplying breakfast needs only. Some of the choristers and their wives saw the potential for lunch, or at least a snack. Doggy bags were hastily assembled from serviettes and sausages and bacon, and perhaps the occasional croissant, was lovingly placed in handbags for a tourist trip around the beauty spots. It would all come in handy.

The experienced staff had seen it all before but this week, Juan, a new waiter, was witnessing the circus for the first time. Each morning his mouth opened a little wider in wonder, as he observed the daily scrum for scrambled egg. Towards the end of the week, and after an especially fraught breakfast, it seemed the toast machine, in sympathy with the put-upon waiting staff, was on a go-slow. Juan approached me and asked the question which had formed in his mind and bothered him for so long. His small frame straightened up and he made himself as tall as possible. Scratching his chin he looked up and asked, "Is Wales in Africa?" Not waiting for an answer he smiled, and, chuckling to himself, walked away.

Is Juan convinced these people are facing starvation in their own country and are stocking up before they return to famine ravaged Wales I wondered. His eyesight might be called into question if this were the case, as very few choristers look as if they are on starvation diets. Or perhaps he was having a joke at my expense.

In our early years of organizing choir tours to Spain we often took our choirs for an evening 'Welcome to Spain' meal. Depending on the size of the group, these evenings were often held in a lovely little restaurant called La Florida which was run by Lolita and Antonio, who became great friends of mine. Unusually for the Spanish Costas, La Florida was popular with both Spanish and ex-pat alike. The restaurant only served food in the evenings. Each morning, Lolita would arrive early at the restaurant to clean the place ready for the evening meals. I would sometimes pop in and help with the chairs and share a coffee with her. It was these conversations that initially helped improve my Spanish.

The restaurant was situated opposite an apartment complex where we accommodated some of the choirs on a self-catering basis. This arrangement was not always ideal for those men who had made the trip with their wives. These guys would be dragged off to the supermarket, where they would buy food and prepare it back in their flats. For those who were permanently single or travelling on their own, it was another story. The morning after the welcome meal, those who could focus properly, spotted from their balconies that the restaurant door was open and, seeing Lolita going about her business, in they marched. Lolita and Antonia were somewhat taken aback when the singers ordered full English breakfasts. Neither Lolita nor Antonio spoke much English, and certainly no Welsh. Lolita later confessed to me they originally thought our happy group of choristers were Russian. It was the fact they appeared 'happy' that told them this wasn't so! Antonio, who resembled an eccentric, but swarthy, English professor with his large bald head, hedged by tufts of hair, set to work. At first there were just four for breakfast. The next morning the numbers grew to ten, then 20. When word got out, La Florida was packed every morning. And all the time Antonio and Lolita smiled and served the choir, and the choir just assumed the restaurant was supposed to be open, when in fact it was only open because they were there cleaning.

Just as I learned more of the language from those morning conversations with Lolita, the choir members learnt the Spanish custom of mid-morning coffee and brandy. It's a fact that they picked this up far more quickly than I picked up the language. What some failed to understand, however, was that the Spanish normally limit that early consumption to one brandy, along with a cup of coffee. After becoming too familiar with the coffee and brandy elevenses, it has been known for certain choristers to take to the other Spanish custom, the afternoon siesta.

Antonio's restaurant was also famous for his paella, which was enjoyed by locals and tourists. As a totally dedicated and addicted smoker of cigarettes he would smoke and cook. Despite the odd intrusion of ash, his paella was legendary throughout the region. Who knows? Perhaps the ash was his secret ingredient.

It is interesting to note what people have learnt over the years from cultural visits to other countries. When I was young and long before I arranged tours for choirs, I visited Spain several times. On one occasion, as a young man, en route to our apartment after a night out, we found ourselves in a scruffy Spanish bar at 4 o'clock in the morning. Just as we were about to finally drag ourselves home, in walked several fishermen who had been out in their boats all night trawling the waters for fish. Suddenly the place which had been fairly empty except for a few homeward-bound Brits, filled up with rowdy, gnarled, old fishermen. Someone would play the guitar and these hard-working men of all ages, shapes and sizes, would stay at the bar for a large part of the morning before they went home for a sleep, prior to returning to sea for their next evening shift.

Thinking of what I have learnt from trips abroad, apart from learning to avoid this particular bar, I suppose the most important thing is that we shouldn't prejudge anyone. How we choose to relax and socialize isn't necessarily everyone's cup of tea, or brandy and Coke, or whisky, or water.

On one tour, a chorister decided that the organized boat trip followed by a beach barbecue was not for him. Instead, he took himself off onto the nearby beaches in search of mussels. He eventually found them at a beach bar. Having personally visited the location on another occasion, it would be more accurate to describe it as a grubby shack rather than bestow on it the grander title of beach bar.

Later that night our intrepid chorister also discovered that Gastro Enteritis was not the president of Spain. Fortunately he recovered from the illness. Unfortunately, it took him nearly eight weeks. At least he lost weight.

There are so many elements to make a choir tour a success. The travel, sightseeing, hospitality of host choirs and the audiences at the concerts are all vital. But right up there in order of importance is the quality of the food and drink which is served up for the visiting choir.

For a tour of Cornwall, the local male voice choir organized a reception and welcome party for our choir in a Falmouth pub. As it was the first night, they gave every Welsh chorister a free Cornish pasty. It was a nice traditional touch and was ravenously and gratefully received by the visitors from across the Severn.

The next day, Saturday, our choristers were the guests of the local rugby club. At lunch time, they were all given a free pint and a Cornish pasty. After they had eaten, the choir sang the Welsh national anthem. This was followed, before the whistle to start the match, with their rendition of 'Trelawney', the anthem of the Cornish 'nation', a call to arms for 20,000 Cornishmen which, at least to my uneducated ear, sounds not unlike the 'Grand Old Duke of York'. Half time and another pint and another Cornish pasty were gratefully received.

The next day the choir was taken for a tour of the county.

The tour finished at Land's End where they were all presented with... a Cornish pasty.

The next evening, our Welsh choir sang with a Cornish choir in an exciting concert which was well received by the audience. Afterwards both choirs, and some of the audience, those who were gluttons for punishment, got together for an afterglow. The beer and music flowed and the management decided that as a special treat for the Welsh choir they should be given a free pint and... a Cornish pasty!

The next day, choir members were taken for a boat trip and as they disembarked at the end of the river jaunt, they were told to follow the organizer to the quayside pub so they could collect their free pint and... a Cornish pasty. Ninety-year-old Dai took matters into his own hands. As a left-wing activist he had battled for all kinds of causes and fought a number of oppressors. But even he couldn't face another pasty, Cornish or otherwise. Sitting away from the rest of the choir as everyone politely accepted another pasty, Dai ordered steak and chips. As the rest of the group persevered with the usual fare, Dai waved his stick and announced to the assembled throng, "I never want to see another 'effin Cornish pasty as long as I live." On the trip back home, the coach stopped in Truro and everyone had Cornish fish and chips.

However unpalatable the glut of Cornish pasties became, they could not have been anywhere near as bad as the plate of nuts a chorister tasted in Spain. During a particularly liquid afterglow he complained to the rest of the choir that the nuts were rock hard and lacked taste. Despite his complaints, he continued to eat from the constantly replenished dish. Having watched him struggle through the 'nuts' for most of the evening, his mates eventually broke the news, that he was eating the olive pips which everyone else had spat out after eating the actual olive. That's what friends are for.

It is not just the Welsh who struggle with the food offered to them in Spain or Cornwall, or anywhere else. Spanish choirs visiting Britain often have difficulty getting used to our food and, like Welsh choirs abroad, they sometimes take matters into their own hands. When one Spanish choir stayed at a Swansea hotel, they asked the manager for a large room with tables and chairs. Chris, the manager, obliged, opened up the bar and looked forward to some brisk trade. He was horrified when he saw the Spanish choristers enter the room with boxes and bags crammed full of hams, meats and chorizos which they had brought from Spain, plus several bottles of wine. After all, this was a licensed hotel, more than capable of supplying and selling its own food and drink. In the end, Chris fought his negative feelings, produced three bottles of whisky from behind the bar, plonked them on one of the tables and in the spirit of 'if you can't beat them join them', he and his staff joined the party. A wonderful afternoon was had by all.

One of the elements of British culture the Spanish do not understand is how individuals can look forward to going out in the evening with the sole purpose of drinking, perhaps even getting drunk. They have a more social view of eating and drinking, which is why they wanted a room in the hotel, rather than head for Swansea city centre in search of multiple hangovers and headaches. It is also why some of the Spanish carried pen knives. It's in case they needed to cut meat or slice some chorizo, or pluck figs from Mumbles' trees.

This habit can cause problems if they venture into British pubs. The members of one choir could not understand why the bouncers got so agitated when they searched them and found that several of the men were carrying Swiss Army knives. Although the Spanish and their knives were prevented from gaining entry, the knives came in handy when we took them for a tour of the Gower peninsula. At Caswell Bay they ran onto the beach, pulled out their knives and headed for the rocks. For the next 30 minutes or so, they sliced away at all the limpets they could find, and then ate them. As I looked at what they were retrieving from the seashore, I was seriously worried for their health. I shouldn't have been concerned, because as far as I know, all the members of that particular choir survived the trip and most are still with us.

The Spanish knife problem was not confined to Wales. It also surfaced in London.

During a security check at the Houses of Parliament, despite being repeatedly told not to carry them, several knives were found in the pockets of another Spanish choir. The knives were, of course, of the pen knife variety and the sole purpose of each knife was to peel the oranges they obviously expected to find growing on London's trees.

Having once been to a match at Valencia's football stadium and been somewhat alarmed to be seated by a group of local fans brandishing knives, I shouldn't have been shocked by this Spanish custom. My new friends at the football shared their sausages, cheese, bread and wine with me and I was most certainly a supporter of CF Valencia by the end of the match.

If knives were a problem with Spanish choirs touring Britain, it was a very different difficulty posed by choirs from Finland. Many people in Britain assume that the Finns are awkward and cold, like icebergs. However, I found that once you break through, they melt and are good fun, and several have become great friends. It was not their sense of humour I battled against, but the fact that before a concert, several choristers insisted I frogmarch them down to the nearest pub. Dressed ready to go on stage, and desperately trying to avoid their female musical director, they would insist on downing a pint before curtain up. One bass baritone insisted on having two pints – one for each leg. Once all the glasses were empty and down on the bar, I would help them scurry back to the church or concert hall where they were performing.

In the past few years, with the onslaught of technology, as in every walk of life, some choristers are hooked on using their mobile phones every minute of the day. A rather self-important member of a choir was always talking about his state-of-the-art new mobile phone. This was the era when, although just becoming popular, mobile phones were nowhere near as common as they are today and in those days were even something of a luxury. This guy never stopped bragging about the cars he owned, the holidays he took and how clever he was. One of his most repeated questions to people standing anywhere near him was, "Have I shown you my new mobile phone?" This particular model was slightly smaller than a house brick.

One afternoon we had arranged a picnic for the choir members. Mobile phone man decided he was not interested in the food we had laid on. Instead, he headed for a nearby food shack and joined us with a takeaway chicken. It was one of those tricky, messy portions, a spit-roast chicken, dripping with various gooey juices and sauces. Delicious, or should have been. The only way to eat the chicken was to tear it apart with your fingers. Not a meal for those who like to remain clean, neat and tidy while they eat.

The joker in the choir pack, seeing the potential for all kinds of dilemmas, borrowed a Spanish mobile phone and concealed himself behind a tree, from where he would be able to watch the drama unfold. Just as Mr Self-Important lifted the chicken to his lips, his friend would ring him. Hands full of greasy, dripping chicken, Mr Self-Important's phone rang. Rummaging for tissues he would try to clean himself as quickly as possible. The moment he raised the phone to his head and was just ready to say hello, his friend behind the tree would ring off. After the first two calls – number withheld, he announced to the other choristers that he was expecting an important message and this was probably his office in Madrid, trying to contact him. Five times the call came just when his hands or mouth, or all three, were full of chicken. By the sixth call Mr Self-Important had not only lost his temper, but had also run out of tissues. His chicken was getting cold and had somewhat lost its appeal. His shirt, hands and special mobile were plastered in grease. The friend behind the tree and the rest of his colleagues were doubled up with laughter. On returning home, I am not sure if Mr Self-Important stayed with the choir.

It is, of course, often difficult to keep everyone happy. Sometimes, something will upset or annoy someone.

*

While there is an element of stress organizing trips and feeling responsible for dozens, sometimes hundreds of people, most visits are memorable and bring happy feelings flooding back. Our trip to the place of the Giant Paella was such a visit.

The inhabitants of Aguas de Busot were proud of their new cultural centre and auditorium. When planning a grand opening for the new premises, they discovered that a party from Wales was soon to visit the area. On this occasion, I was due to be accompanying a trip for a mixed group of performers. A friendly, gushing letter from the town to my colleagues in Spain asked if we would honour the town by performing at their official grand opening. We had to decline as we were not due to arrive in Spain until three weeks after the planned event. Although it might seem like it on occasions, we hadn't at that stage mastered the art of being in two places at the same time.

"Don't worry," said the town mayor, "we'll postpone the opening until you arrive."

"Sorry. No good," we replied "we already have a charity concert on that Sunday evening."

"Don't worry," said the mayor, "we'll hold it on the Sunday afternoon, buy you lunch and pay for the buses to take you back in time for your charity concert."

So it was that one fine Sunday morning we arrived at

the seemingly sleepy town of Aguas de Busot. Two coaches parked and tipped out our collection of Welsh talent which, on this occasion included a group of young Welsh dancers and their parents, a ladies' choir who performed only in Welsh, various harpists and a bloody great harp, pianists and assorted hungover folk musicians.

The buses parked above the town in a street near the school. Looking down, we had a perfect view of the centre where we would be performing. Some of the young dancers were intrigued by what they saw in the school yard. Several men were standing around what looked like a huge round boat, rather like a giant coracle. The men were brandishing giant paddling oars and moving them in and out of the boat. It took a while before we realised that the boat was in fact a massive wok. The men were using the oars to stir the huge paella which was going to be our lunch.

The civic opening of the culture centre was a great success and all the participants performed brilliantly. The whole event was done respectfully and with dignity. Except that is, for the split-second when one of our hungover musicians woke and couldn't stop himself from making a bawdy comment at the very moment the centre was officially opened. In his defence, it should be pointed out that the ribbon was cut by the mayor's amazingly attractive daughter. And she did bend forward to complete the task. I think we got away with that momentary lapse of etiquette and an international incident was mercifully avoided.

The event ended with a joint piece from the local choir and band. At the end, the local town band marched on to the school, trumpets blaring, and we followed them to the huge marquee which had been erected in the school grounds. Dozens of tables were heaving with wine, water, soft drinks, meats, cheeses, potatoes and salads. Pride of place was afforded to the gigantic paella which we had seen from above. Standing next to it we could now see it in all its culinary glory.

"Are those things snails?"

"Course not."

"Is that rabbit or chicken?"

"I'm sure it's chicken."

"Ugh, I hate prawns."

"The rice is nice, though."

During lunch, the town band played and our singers and musicians responded. Then the dancers from the town danced and ours responded. And so it went on, musician and dancer matched by musician and dancer. It was like something out of 'Dueling Banjos' multiplied by 200. It was a wonderful afternoon and proof, if any were needed, that the Spanish know how to throw a party.

On our way to the evening concert we took a leaf out of a Finnish choir's book of concert etiquette. However, our desire to find a bar was fuelled by a love of rugby rather than alcohol. We eventually found the only bar along the coast showing the Wales versus England rugby match being played at Wembley. Sadly, unlike the Finns, we were late for the concert. It was all down to Scott Gibbs and Neil Jenkins. Gibbs scored a magnificent last-gasp try to beat the English. There was no way we could miss the conversion and (praise be to God), neither did Neil Jenkins.

It was a never-to-be-forgotten day. Neither will the paella ever be forgotten. Musicians being musicians, they polished it off along with everything else that was going free. The ladies and the young people, probably because their imagination is more fertile, and they had seen the oars and men poking around in the food, gave the paella a miss. Nothing to do with the seafood... and who mentioned the snails? For them we had to stop for burgers on the way home. Personally, I took my chances with the paella.

Joke from the Coach I

Huw's ship had sunk and he, the only survivor, found himself washed up on a deserted island.

A religious man, Huw decided to pass the time until rescue by building a church.

Five long years had passed and the church was complete – Noddfa, a magnificent structure, especially when one considers the lack of tools.

A couple of weeks later and boredom had once again set in. "What shall I do now," said Huw who had taken to arguing with himself. "I know, I'll build a church," he said to nobody in particular. And so Huw set about building another church.

Six years passed before Tabernacle was finished. After all, Huw was older and slower, and good staff were hard to find. It was bound to take longer to build.

Almost twelve months later, Huw was rescued at last. His rescuers were amazed to find two churches on a desert island. Not unreasonably, the ship's captain asked Huw, "Why build two churches?"

"WHY?" asked Huw incredulously. "Because I don't go to that one," said Huw, pointing at Noddfa.

First human contact in over twelve years and the first thing they do is ask a bloody stupid question! Huw wondered if he should stay on the island.

CHAPTER 4

Lost in Translation

FOOD AND DRINK always play a major part of any choir
tour. Perhaps the most demanding part of organizing
a trip is the fact that food-wise, you are taking one culture
to another. Between Wales and Spain, or indeed between
anywhere and anywhere else in the world, so much can be
lost in translation.

It is claimed, with some justification, that the strength
of a small nation lies with its language and its culture, and
that language is one of our greatest tools for creating culture
and making friends. Sadly, it can also cause untold problems
when two people from different cultures try to work together.
In America, fanny most definitely does not mean what it
means in Britain. It means backside. A friend offered to help
an American lady struggling to get her shopping into her
car. He asked if she would like him to close the car door and
was surprised when she replied, "It's OK, I'll close it with my
fanny."

Above the bar in an Italian hotel, someone who has not
quite mastered the art of the English language, had written,
'Try our wines. They will leave you with nothing to hope for,'
whilst in a Paris hotel the sign reads, 'Visitors are respectfully
asked to leave all their values at reception.'

Organising trips abroad, I have seen some 'interesting'
faux pas. The menu at a Spanish restaurant offered 'huevos

revueltos'. This should have appeared on the board as scrambled eggs. Unfortunately, the translator offered the public 'revolting' eggs.

Elsewhere in Spain, a town decided it was time they produced publicity booklets for English-speaking tourists. Forty thousand were printed and distributed. It wasn't long (but too late to do anything about it) before someone noticed the classic error. The bright glossy booklet began with a friendly greeting to English speakers from across Europe. Instead of the two words, 'Dear Friend', it read, 'Dear *Fiend*'.

One party of male voice choristers had mixed feelings when they arrived at the hotel which had been booked. Ready to sign in for the stay, some were worried while others grew more excited by the minute. Wear and tear and possible bad weather had resulted in several letters on the flashing neon sign failing to work. The E, L and the final O were missing from the Hotel Tito's welcome. It meant they were booking in for a stay at the Hot Tit. On one level it should have boosted the number of residents, but it only succeeded in embarrassing the owner. He was a member of the local council, possibly in charge of education. He soon realised the faulty sign failed to set the best example for young impressionable minds learning English.

It is not just signs that pose linguistic problems. If one's grasp of a language is poor then all kinds of misunderstandings can develop. One evening the male voice choir was relaxing in a Spanish bar near their hotel. An extremely well-dressed man called Diego was passing through the group handing out business cards. The card was written in several languages but surprisingly not English, or Welsh. Combining their collective ignorance, the choristers decided it must be an invitation to another bar. Gwynfor, who had once visited Benidorm, was not satisfied by the group's assumptions and called for the help of a local. Gwynfor was convinced the man he had chosen spoke fluent English, but when he began to translate, it soon became clear that Gwynfor was mistaken. Undeterred, he concentrated all the more and by the end of the interpreter's pigeon English, he was convinced he had the drift of what was on offer.

"Him over there, that bloke there," said Gwynfor pointing to Diego, who still seemed to be doing a brisk trade distributing his free business cards to others in the bar, "well that bloke, right, has invited us to his bar and will give us all a free drink so long as we sing for him and his customers." Gwynfor even mentioned that the leader of the choir would be allowed a freebie. No-one was quite sure what Diego or Gwynfor meant by that. No-one worried, it was time to call taxis and get down there as fast as possible.

We arrived at the bar just as Gwynfor was ushering people in to the second taxi. I was able to encourage the ageing chapel boys out of the vehicle with the news that Diego's place was not a bar, but a well-known local brothel.

Unfortunately, Stephen, the choir's musical director, curious to discover what his freebie would be, had gone on in the first taxi, accompanied by his boyfriend, second tenor, Nigel. Most definitely a wasted evening for Stephen and Nigel, and sadly also for the beautiful Brazilian girls who worked at 'Diego's Place', and certainly no freebies.

Whilst music is a universal language and there are never any communication problems when our choirs are singing, the problems start when people try to speak to each other. I have always felt sorry for those who try to learn English. There are times when it seems to have no rhyme or reason to it. Imagine a foreign student trying to come to terms with the language. Shown the bough of a tree, he now knows that O U G H is pronounced OW. So when he sees the word COUGH he has every reason to tell his friends that he thinks he is developing a nasty COW in his chest. His landlady spreads out the DOUGH to make bread, so after his encounter with a cough he now realises she is using DOFF, but of course it's pronounced DOE. At this point he has every right to tell us he has had ENOE of this crazy lingo. Then we would have to correct him and tell him he has had ENUFF.

Seeing the problems my first language can cause, I have every sympathy for the Spanish landlady who used to practise her English on me. She got terribly mixed up with the words sheep, sheet and shit. I first realised her difficulty when she informed me that she had put another shit on my bed to keep me warm.

While Welsh choir members struggle in other countries, it must be even worse when people from abroad come to Wales. Not only do they have to battle with the unpredictability of English, but they now have the added challenge of bilingual signs in Welsh and English. A Finnish friend, whom I had originally met through a touring Finnish choir, decided he should add Welsh to the list of languages he spoke. He had arranged to stay in our home and telephoned to say he would not be long. I was very impressed when he told me that he had just passed a sign telling him 'Gwasanaethau', was one mile away. Gwasanaethau was pronounced perfectly. However, about 30 minutes later he rang again. This time his voice sounded anxious.

"I must have been mistaken," he said. "I seem to be going away from you, in the opposite direction. A few minutes ago the town of Gwasanaethau was one mile away. Now it's 25.' Gwasanaethau is, of course, the Welsh word for services, or in this case, motorway services.

His problem was similar to an English friend who whilst being driven around north Wales, noticed several signs outside houses, proclaiming AR WERTH. "My Goodness," he said after a while, "These estate agents A. R. Worth have got a real monopoly around here haven't they?" (AR WERTH is For Sale.)

Similarly some American friends rang to say that the Gwesty Hotel chain seems to have cornered the market in Wales. (Gwesty is the Welsh word for hotel.)

Stories of confusion caused by the use of wrong words are not unique to people from other countries. The Welsh abroad can also excel in this and I confess I have made the occasional embarrassing mistake.

Returning home late and having lost his key, one young chorister tried to climb into the apartment complex, fell, and badly cut his thigh. We called an ambulance and as I was the only person in the party who spoke any Spanish, I accompanied him to the hospital. At this stage my Spanish was very rocky, as I had only just started learning. So I spent the entire journey to the hospital worrying about what would happen when we arrived.

For 20 minutes I rummaged around in my brain and then practised how I would say, "He's very drunk, he's fallen and has a terrible cut on his left leg."

At the hospital, we were met by a distinguished-looking surgeon. In my over rehearsed Spanish, I told him that the chorister was very drunk and had a terrible cut on his left leg. The surgeon responded in perfect English.

"Well that is a coincidence. He has a terrible cut on his right leg also."

I suppose if I struggle to recognise my left from my right in my mother tongue, then I have very little chance of getting it right in Spanish.

On another occasion, and in a different Spanish town, a chorister was walking through a particularly unpleasant area. It was 2 a.m. and, more than slightly the worse for wear, he decided to take a short cut back to our hotel. Suddenly, he was aware of a large Eastern European brandishing a knife. Although drunk, our chorister quickly realised the man was not a top tenor and certainly not part of a welcoming committee. Next, our chorister was pushed into a garage doorway and threatened with a knife. Our man handed over his watch and what money he hadn't drunk.

When he got back to the hotel, although it was past 2 a.m., the chorister stormed to my room and woke me up. He was understandably distraught. I was afraid he would wake everyone up and the only way to calm him down was by pouring him another drink. We eventually agreed that I would immediately accompany him to the *Guardia Civil*, so that he could report the crime.

Some Spanish people find the *Guardia Civil* difficult. To visit any kind of police station at that time in the morning is an unpleasant experience. Having woken him up, the officer who took our statement was particularly displeased to see us.

The officers and their families lived over the police station and the whole building felt in need of cleaning and a lick, or several licks, of paint. In the interview room, the stench of urine and vomit wafted up from the cells. Annoyed that we had disturbed his sleep, he tried to encourage us to book a translator, and return at a more civilized hour, but that would have cost us many Euros, and meant a return journey. Instead, I battled on with my fledgling grasp of the language and explained what had happened. The only time we got anything resembling eye contact was after I had explained that the chorister had been threatened with a knife. Feeling intimidated by the policeman's attitude, I managed to mix my *cucharas* with my *cuchillos*. *Cuchara* is a spoon, while *cuchillo* is a knife. The policeman stared at me with a mix of boredom, anger and incredulity. He then asked for clarification as he wanted to know whether my friend had really been threatened by a spoon-wielding Eastern European. Somehow it just doesn't strike the same amount of terror as being coerced by a knife. But the police report definitely refers to the dangers of attacks by a spoon. Fortunately, the insurance company understood our dilemma and no doubt enjoyed a laugh at our expense.

On these organized trips, I am not alone in managing to mix ideas and select the wrong words. I would be a rich man if I were given a £1 every time someone confused Flamingos and Flamenco. It always brings a smile to my face when I'm asked if there is any chance of taking the choir members to see the flamingos dance. The mistake forces all types of images into my head, such as flamenco dancers knee-deep in the salt lakes, and flamingos, castanets clacking, pecking and strutting their way through a dance routine in a hotel.

Unfamiliarity with a language often results in people being set up by those who are fluent speakers.

Cyril was very nervous about touring with the choir in a country where everyone would be speaking a language he didn't understand. Discounting a trip to Liverpool in 1966 to renew his dog license, he had never before been abroad.

One evening he was relaxing in a bar with his friends from the choir. They had already consumed several pints between them and, as in many Spanish bars, they had opened a tab. The arrangement was that they would pay at the end. Feeling the nervousness that had engulfed him before he left Wales, Cyril had earlier asked one of his chorister friends to write down on a piece of paper what he would have to say to the barman to order the drinks.

Although he practised, when he arrived at the bar, his courage deserted him and he handed the piece of paper to the barmaid. She read it and immediately called the bar manager who began shouting and threatening to call the police. Cyril was flabbergasted. Admittedly he wasn't expecting a proposal of marriage from the barmaid, but Cyril was at least expecting a smile and some pleasant chit chat in another language.

As they had been drinking for some time, the barmaid anticipated that Cyril would be paying the not inconsiderable tab. Therefore she was horrified to read the note, which read *Lo siento – No Tengo Dinero* (I am sorry I have no money). Alarmed, the bar manager made straight for the group of

Bryncoch Male Voice Choir in Torrevieja, Spain, 1995 – our first choir tour.

Singing in the town square can often help attract an audience to the church concert.

Cardiff Blues Choir not exactly singing the blues at La Iglesia Inmaculada Concepcion, Torrevieja.

Men in skirts – what did the Spaniards think of our Celtic cousins from Aberfeldy – and what does a Scotsman wear under his kilt? We got the answer at the post-concert ceilidh!

"Where is the Prince of Wales when you need him?"

Where is Alfonso in this photograph?

The audience appreciates the performance.

Fond memories at Torrevieja's Monument to the Choirs.

Spanish lessons with Lolita, Antonio and friends who prepared full breakfasts of bacon and eggs for our choir, despite the restaurant being closed in the mornings.

As chaplain of the Costa Blanca, Welshman 'Father' Eric was a great supporter of our Welsh choirs in Spain, but even he might have thought twice about inviting the whole group to lunch at his lovely Costa Blanca home!

"Does the number 17 bus to Cwmavon stop here?"

"Hey, buttie, no wonder it was so cheap to get into the Camp Nou, Barcelona are playing away!"

"It's not much of a castle, but for now it's ours," say an invading Welsh choir. I think the Spanish got these invaders to leave the country rather easier than Charlton Heston's El Cid when he tried to clear the Moors from Spain.

Pretty in pink: Is it flamenco or flamingo?!

Memorial concert at Torrevieja's Palacio de la Musica in honour of the maestro Ricardo Lafuente, affectionaly known as Dicky Fountain by all Welsh people who were lucky enough to meet him. Sadly missed.

Cecilio Gallego – musician and friend – tragically murdered by a bomb blast whilst returning from a family lunch. The bomb exploded in a bus stop outside the local *Guardia Civil* station in Santa Pola.

Dawnswyr Penrhyd – Wales' very best young dancers shaking a leg in Tuscany.

The committee of Kyrkslätts Manskör, a choir from Finland's Swedish-speaking community, visit the Lord Mayor of Swansea.

Kyrkslätts Manskör choir. Like most Finns, many speak English, but some have now learnt Welsh too.

Craig and Leah dance and Richard plays for the British ambassador in Helsinki.

A poster of their visit to France in 2011.

Wherever they go in the world, the Ogmore Male Voice Choir are always prepared. They have a flag for every destination and occasion.

Melbourne-based Australian Welsh Male Choir perform at the village church in Melbourne, Derbyshire, home of the original Lord Melbourne.

The Australian Welsh Male Choir at the Millennium Centre, Cardiff, March 2012.

Craig, a popular member of the Australian Welsh Male Choir.

Spanish choir with Swansea's Lord Mayor at the Brangwyn Hall.

Ricardo Lafuente, a great man, meets another great man at the Tower of London.

The Spanish Armada – Coros y Orquesta La Salinas de Torrevieja arrive at the Tower of London.

drinkers and was only reassured when he saw the colour of their money. He soon realised that they had played a trick on poor Cyril. Very quickly he allowed the drinkers to continue pushing the tab higher and higher.

Cyril did venture to the bar again to order more drinks, but not immediately. He also struck up a firm friendship with the barmaid... eventually, but certainly there was no proposal of marriage or anything else.

On one occasion a beautiful young Welsh soprano accompanying a male voice choir in Helsinki inadvertently set herself up for a spot of linguistic confusion. Sitting in the bar with the choristers, it was her night off, so she decided to examine the cocktail list. After much study she made her way to the bar. Clutching the list rather shyly and, as quietly as possible, she gave the barman her order. Sadly, her voice was not as quiet as she'd hoped. Childish giggling surfaced from our group as they heard her ask if it would be possible to have 'Sex on the beach'. She returned to her seat and the cocktail duly arrived. Once she had finished, another drink appeared. She was determined not to get carried away as she was singing in a concert the following evening. Deciding against any more 'Sex on the Beach', she bade the choir members good night and retired to bed.

The next evening the choir and soprano performed brilliantly and afterwards returned in triumph to the bar which was now packed. The previously discreet barman suddenly seemed to have developed a huge booming baritone voice. Spotting our soprano, he bellowed across the crowded room, "You want sex on the beach tonight?" Exit stage left, one shy, embarrassed, young soprano.

Spain has its own brand of whisky whose name, to the English ear, is every bit as suggestive as 'Sex on the Beach'. It is called Dyk, which is pronounced Dick. I have seen many choristers, new to Spain, stand at the bar totally nonplussed when asked in broken English, "You want large dick?" Most male choristers, and indeed most female choristers, see the funny side of the question, while others treat it as a serious attack on their macho image!

"Whisky, please."

"You want big Dyk?"

"Wot you say?"

"Would sir like a big Dyk?"

Commotion ensues at the bar.

"Muriel, come 'ere luv. We is goin'. I is not staying in this place."

It is not just through words that visitors to another country can feel as if everything is lost in translation. The feeling can often intensify when individuals try to cope with the traditions of another country. We organized a tour of south Wales and London for a choir and orchestra from Spain. After an enjoyable week in Wales we set off for London. On our first night in the hotel bar the doors burst open and in came three young male members of the orchestra. To the accompaniment of music on a CD, they tiptoed into the bar making balletic pirouette movements. If this seems bizarre, it gets worse. Each one of the musicians wore a kilt. Determined not to reveal all, and prove what a Spaniard wears under his kilt, they had to hold the kilt down as they made their ballet movements. By the end of the music, the impromptu audience had forgotten their initial shock and felt the whole event had been fun. We all had one question for them. What made them come to Wales and London, dressed in kilts?

It all started back in Spain where they had been watching television. Prince Charles appeared on the screen wearing a kilt. He was the Prince of Wales, so therefore all Welsh people must wear kilts. On the strength of that assumption and at some cost, the three lads commissioned three kilts. It was only when they arrived in Wales that they realised their mistake. No-one was wearing a kilt. Embarrassed by their mistake they eventually confided in the only Welsh person they actually knew – me. The boys decided to wait until they reached London, before donning the kilts. We were all impressed that, despite being so wrong about the national costume, they had carried the situation so well. Mind you, there are people who will offer an argument that the kilt is a Welsh national garment, but that is another story.

The Spanish kilt performance was nowhere near as outrageous as that given by a Scottish choir in Spain. After a successful concert they marched to the reception at the *Ayuntamiento* (Town hall) straight through the evening market, dressed in kilts, headed by two pipers, also in full costume. The startled look on the faces of market traders and shoppers, suggested the locals had no idea how they should react to this fearsome bunch of men in skirts, while all the women in the group seemed to be wearing trousers!

Later that evening our Scottish friends sat outside a bar being happily observed by the local police, who seemed to be enjoying what was obviously an entertaining interlude. As time passed and drink loosened the Scottish inhibitions, the guys started wheeling and circling to the sound of the music. As the kilts swirled around, it seemed the age-old question was about to be answered, "What do Scotsmen wear under their kilt?"

This was when the police decided it was time to stop smiling, move across the road and have a word with the revelers. The Scots were gently escorted back to their hotel, kilts in place, but minus bagpipes, which we retrieved the following day.

*

It is not just our traditional costumes which can pose problems for Spanish people. They might rule the world with football, but rugby is a relatively unknown game to most Spanish people, especially women.

Many years ago I travelled on the train to the old Cardiff Arms Park for an international between Wales and England. I had three tickets, one for me and one each for David and Maria, my friends from Spain. We were accompanied by several members of a Welsh choir many of whom were without a ticket, but travelling in hope. At such a time you don't want anyone with a ticket to let the side down by expressing ignorance of the sport. There is no surer way of igniting the wrath of those who know their sport, but have no way of getting into the match. Unfortunately, Maria did just that. In good English, but far too loudly she said, "Tell me, I think I have seen rugby on television, but can you remind me what type of bat they use?"

Cultural confusion can also be spread by the press. A visiting choir was due to sing in a Welsh town with a local choir. However, long before they arrived, the scheduled concert was rearranged for the following day. Despite the fact that everyone was happy with the new arrangements, we were all slightly worried when we read the headline in the local paper, 'Tonight's Concert is on Tomorrow'.

When booking flights and hotels for choirs we have to go through the choir list with a proverbial toothcomb. The Welsh have invented their own culture of nicknames. It is not surprising when you consider how many Joneses, Evanses and Davieses there are in a land of 3,000,000. In one Welsh village a retired coal miner was called Dai Nine Months. When I asked how he acquired the name, I discovered he had been involved in an underground explosion. Sadly, he lost a quarter of his ear. This meant he was left with three-quarters of an ear. In many parts of Wales people pronounce the twelve-month period as 'ear, dropping the y. So, with a quarter of his lobe missing, he was affectionately known as Dai Nine Months.

When the list of names for a planned tour land on our desk we have to check them against passports. Some of the names we have had to query, include Dai Bottom Bass, Gog Evans, Dai Twp, Daft Harry, and Ginge Thomas. Inevitably, Dai Bungalow makes an appearance. He is usually the chorister who is regarded as a little slow, so named, because he has nothing upstairs. When we contact the choir leaders and say we need full names to put on the list for the flight company, they often express amazement. As far as they are concerned these are their proper names.

*

A large Welsh male voice choir, complete with wives, girlfriends and supporters arrived at their Spanish hotel. The special welcome party started as soon as the last guest had checked-in. It soon became apparent that the group was divided into two factions. There were those who had voted for Spain as a tour destination and a vociferous minority, led by the deputy chairman, who were opposed to the idea, and seemingly determined not to have a good time.

Several minutes into the party, a red faced and flustered deputy chairman stormed into the room. Sweating profusely and consulting his watch, he complained loudly and bitterly that he had been stuck in the lift for four minutes.

"Only four minutes?" some of the choir asked.

I appreciate that four minutes in that situation is four minutes too long. However, it soon became clear that being stuck in the lift was not the issue which was making his face bulge and glow redder and redder by the second. His complaint was all to do with who had rescued him. José, the receptionist who checked the choir in, had risen to the occasion and opened the lift doors safely. This was not good enough. Mr Angry had expected to be rescued by a specialist team, whose sole purpose in life was to snatch people from malfunctioning lifts, especially important people, such as the deputy chairman of a Welsh male voice choir. We tried to explain that very few hotels in the world employ a lift rescue team for what is such a rare occurrence. Thinking on his feet, my colleague Graham also pointed out that, as José had proved, the hotel staff were all trained for this eventuality. Mr Angry, soon to become Mr Unpleasant, was having none of it and continued shouting and screaming in front of us and everyone else who was trying to enjoy the party. Nothing we said or did was going to placate him, not even the hotel's generous offer of free drinks. He stormed around the room with a face like thunder, telling everyone who would listen what a terrible time he was having and what a gargantuan mistake the choir had made in booking this place. By now, Mr Deputy Chairman had been in the hotel approximately 20 minutes, four of which had been spent in the lift. Despite his negative feelings he did graciously accept the offer of free drinks... again and again. His attitude was turning the evening into a stressful event. When his formidable looking wife approached, I feared the worst. Watching her weave from side to side as she tried to make the straight line from her to me, I realised she too had accepted the free drinks. She tottered in front of me, her eyes focusing through the haze. I feared the worst.

"Don't worry luv," she said, "it's probably his piles playing him up. Order me another Martini will you? And then introduce me to Pablo, the bar manager. He's gorgeous!"

*

After the 9/11 atrocities, security heightened at all airports. One choir had waited for ages to clear customs, but once clear, they found their flight delayed. With a couple of hours to kill before boarding the plane, they were not too disappointed. After all they were on tour... and the wives were at home. In these situations there are only so many times you can walk around a shop and look at the same unwanted gifts and the same unreadable books and magazines. "Time for a pint then," said Penry, who liked to think he was the choir's ideas man. "Might get two in," said Maldwyn, Penry's apprentice in crime. Motion carried, the choristers' established base camp in one of the airport bars. It wasn't long before the songs began to flow alongside everything else that was flowing from pumps and bottles. Soon, no doubt attracted by the singing, there were a number of nationalities represented inside that bar. It was quite a challenge for the choir to match 'Sospan Fach' with Bahrain or 'Myfanwy' with Baghdad. Despite the challenges, the boys seemed to succeed in spanning the cultural divide and it wasn't long before they received requests to sing particular songs (as opposed to requests to leave the bar).

As more and more customers joined in the fun, there was an increase in the number of requests from the passengers. As ever, the choir entered into the mood of the moment and the choristers were thoroughly enjoying the fact that so many strangers were asking for their favourite song. "Good job we don't have a concert for a couple of nights," said the musical director.

And so it was that some two hours after the scheduled departure time, our happy band of choristers were disturbed by both the bar manager and the accompanying tannoy announcement along the lines of, "As much as we have all enjoyed the impromptu singing during the delay of flight number XXX, would the Welsh choir please proceed with some haste to departure gate number 17, where their flight is boarding and the gate will soon be closing".

I had never seen so many elderly, overweight, out of condition men, move so quickly. We all had to make a run for the plane and they couldn't "dilly-dally on the way". Limbs that hadn't moved for some considerable time had to get cracking, hopefully without cracking, which was becoming a concern.

Safely aboard, there was a hell of a queue for the loo.

As the elderly bladders of the choristers tried to hold out, Dai decided to relieve – if that's the right word – some of the pressure, by attempting to be humorous.

"Why do airline toilets have frosted glass?" he asked, pausing dramatically for the idiocy of his question to sink in. "I mean," he continued, "what is the point? Who's going to look in? No-one's going to get up there are they? If they do manage to get up to that height, then perhaps they deserve a peep."

The boys who got the joke pleaded with Dai not to expand on his theory, just in case their bladders started to laugh... or cry!

Evan hadn't laughed at the joke but had sat quietly, looking very serious during Dai's mini speech. Suddenly a penny seemed to drop somewhere inside him. "Oh, I see. Is that what they call the Mile High Club? Membership is for people who go to the toilet in the sky?"

The rest of the choir were in too much discomfort to correct him and there was silent shuffling to the one toilet until eventually everyone was seated for what was, by now, a fairly short flight. Most of the choristers slept soundly and sometimes loudly, until we reached our destination.

This reminds me of a tale told by an Australian choir who argued that they were the world's highest paid choir. Up in the air, word spread of their presence on a flight to Europe. Possibly the sight of 70 elderly gentlemen in choir blazers gave it away. A passenger offered them five dollars if they would sing. They obliged and as they were travelling at 35,000 feet when they were paid the five dollars, they became the world's highest paid choir.

It has been known for me to offer certain choirs a fiver to shut up!

CHAPTER 5

Every Choir has its Characters

THE BEAUTY OF the Welsh choir performance in the airport bar was that it was ad hoc. Spontaneity seems to be a gift which some choirs and individuals possess while others fear it like a dangerous virus.

Ad hoc and spontaneous are not words you would hurl at Michael. Michael lives in Spain and is an excellent singer, musician and musical director. He runs choral workshops for ex-pats and is the musical director of two ex-pat choirs. On one occasion, Michael organized a wonderful concert at a beautiful Spanish church for our visiting ladies' choir and his newly formed ex-pat male voice choir.

Despite being christened Michael, he was known by many as Hilda, after the draconian wife in John Mortimer's *Rumpole of the Bailey*: Hilda, 'she who must be obeyed'.

His closest friends and even his doting mother agreed that, on occasions, Michael could be a pompous ass.

Before their big concert with his choir, our ladies needed to rehearse at the hotel where Hilda was running his latest workshop. They asked if they might borrow his electric piano. After much debate, during which they discovered it was his birthday, Michael agreed that if they turned up at 1 p.m. prompt and sang 'Happy Birthday' he would allow them to use the piano for 20 minutes. The choir arrived at the

73

agreed time, sang 'Happy birthday, dear Michael', in Welsh and then ran through their pieces in 20 minutes, timed to the second by you-know-who. Michael went off to his birthday celebrations, where he regaled everyone prepared to listen with the tale of how he had prepared the ladies' choir from Wales for their next concert. No doubt by the end of the party he had organized the concert, arranged the music, printed the posters and sold all the tickets.

That should have been the end of our story. The choir had their rehearsal and Hilda enjoyed his party and the self-praise he heaped on himself so, in a bizarre way, everyone was happy. However, concluding the story at that point fails to give credit to some of the characters, lurking in the background, who were connected to the choir. Characters such as musical director Annie Walker and her husband 'Grab it all Graham'. Now that they knew where Michael's electric piano was hidden, there was no way the instrument would be allowed to rest in peace. The 'Piano Liberation Party' was duly formed over a few jugs of sangria. In any undercover escapade they, Annie and Graham, would be ably assisted by the choir accompanist Fingers Thomas and The Twins. The twins were individually known as Madcap Moira and Homicide Hilary. They were called the twins because they looked so unlike each other. Homicide Hilary was tall and lithe and wore a nice line in flowered blouses, while Madcap Moira, could generally be best described as a pretty lady in cloth cap and cardigan, five foot nothing of knitted woollen cardigan.

So it was, armed with insider knowledge of where the piano was kept, that Annie Walker and her Piano Liberation Party planned their operation with SAS-style precision. The keys to the room where the piano was stored were easy to obtain. Alfredo, the young security guard, was easily seduced by Madcap Moira and Homicide Hilary, fresh from their Women's Institute flower arranging and seduction course.

With 'Grab it all Graham' as look out, the gang proceeded to the room where the piano was stored and stumbled about in the dark looking for it. In a similar situation, Dr Watson might have said to Holmes, "What's afoot, Sherlock?" For *our* group of adventurers the piano was afoot, as it had actually tumbled on to Madcap's toes. Now that they knew where the piano was, the group moved towards the door.

"All clear, Graham?" they whispered.

There was no answer.

Again they called, a little louder, but still as quietly as possible, "All clear?"

Unfortunately their lookout was suffering from a bout of the runs. He too was stumbling about in the dark, only he was in the ladies' toilet, desperately searching for lights to the gents' toilet. Not knowing where he was, Annie assumed that her husband, Graham, had been caught in the act of piano theft. She knew she could trust him and that he wouldn't break under torture... at least not until his captors realised that for a beer he was anyone's.

The gang continued with their daring raid. Thinking on their feet and already one man and one foot down, Homicide Hilary decided it wouldn't be safe to take the lift to the first floor. Annie, Fingers, Homicide and Madcap Moira struggled manfully and womanfully to carry the piano up the stairs and along a myriad of corridors to the appointed meeting place. Once the rehearsal was finished and after the others had left the room, the gang then had to repeat the struggle and carry the piano back to the place where it was kept. With the job done, they caught their breath by collapsing on top of the piano. As Fingers' body hit the instrument he suddenly hit something else.

"What's this?" he asked, pulling a lever which released wheels. The piano had wheels! Four people let out the loudest communal, "Oh ****," ever heard.

*

Whilst concerts can be made difficult by awkward musical directors, such as Michael/Hilda, problems can also arise from unexpected incidents. My colleague, Graham was the kind of person whose fame was not restricted to his musical prowess. Mention the name Graham and people immediately think of pairs of glasses. He has a history of misplacing his spectacles and a reputation for putting them everywhere, except where they should be. That is, above his nose!

Eventually it was agreed the best solution would be to attach his glasses to a cord and place it around his neck.

During a concert which Graham was presenting, the guest soprano had given a wonderful performance for which she was receiving a well-deserved standing ovation from the packed church audience. Graham turned towards the soprano who was well upholstered and gave her a warm embrace. Once contact was made between Graham's dangling glasses and the soprano's chest, something had to give. Unfortunately, it was Graham's glasses. They never stood a chance and crushed on impact. After his accident with the singer's chest, Graham couldn't see a thing. This was definitely a handicap, as he had written down copious notes to help him introduce the various items. In addition, he had notes in Spanish and English as he had sat down with the MD of the Spanish choir with whom the Welsh choir was sharing the concert. For the rest of the evening he successfully hummed and ha-hed his way through the event and peered out at an audience he couldn't see. At the end of the evening, he too received an ovation and several beers from an embarrassed soprano plus a grateful choir. Ironically, as the beer flowed, Graham's eyesight seemed to improve.

*

It was 'Pete the Pill's' 40th birthday, so when I informed the choir that we would be performing in an old people's home, many of the choristers were keen to stay in their hotel and celebrate with Pete.

They didn't fancy singing to a roomful of people whom they unfairly imagined would be drooling and dribbling, trying to sing along when they didn't know the words. Who knows, perhaps the antipathy to the idea came from the fact that the thought of an old people's home was too close to real life for some of the older fellows in the choir. More likely this afternoon's concert was too close to the morning after the night before. And anyway, it was Pete's birthday.

To be fair, the choir members didn't take too much persuading. As with most choirs, these boys were only too happy to perform for anyone who might be less fortunate than themselves. We explained that the Spanish attitude to old age is very different to ours in the UK. In Spain the homes are often called *Residencias de Tres Edad* which translates as Homes for the Third Age, as opposed to old age.

In Spain there seems to be more respect for the elderly than in the UK. Rather than being shoved in a corner and silenced, as is often the case in Britain, the Spanish old folk are placed on a pedestal and their opinions valued.

In the homes respect is shown to the residents by the staff and they are often lively places where the residents are encouraged to live life to the full.

What's more, many *Residencias* are licensed premises. Holidays and day trips are organized on a regular basis for the residents and certain residencies welcome groups of holidaymakers from other residencies.

Many *Residencias* have their own choir and band and several interest and activity clubs. The passion shown over games of dominoes and cards has to be seen to be believed. Despite my reassuring words, most of the members of our Welsh Valleys choir arrived expecting to sing to the poor old folk in the home. They were totally unprepared for what hit them. Hundreds turned up, most of whom were there by choice.

After the choir had performed, beer and snacks were organised for everyone, as was whisky, brandy, wines, coffees and whatever anyone wanted.

As our group enjoyed the unexpected hospitality another concert started, performed by the *Residencia* performing arts team. They had devised the show especially for our choir, who watched in amazement as ageing flamenco guitarists, flamenco dancers, musicians and dancers served up a never-to-be-forgotten treat. It has to be said that these people were good.

Torrevieja, the town in which the choir were performing, has two salt lakes and the largest lake is dredged for the commodity every day. It is a fact that much of the salt used in northern Europe to grit the roads during harsh winters will come from this area of Spain. A dying breed of local artisans makes beautiful ships from the salt dredged from the lake. These magnificent *Barcas de Sal*, or salt boats, are often used by the town as gifts for visiting dignitaries and celebrities. Indeed some of the craftsmen lived at the *Residencia* we were visiting.

Our choir's musical director was presented with his salt boat mounted in a glass case by one of the female residents. She had been rather noticeable throughout the evening, mainly because she wore a sash. For anyone brave enough to approach her and read the writing on the sash they would realise they were indeed peering at Miss Torrevieja 1956. Our musical director was so startled by her passionate embrace and equally passionate kiss, that he dropped the gift. Fortunately the boat rode the carpet and mercifully there was no broken glass.

The Welsh choristers, having consumed copious amounts of free booze, started to sing again. Miss Torrevieja 1956 accompanied one of the songs with her own version of a flamenco dance. *Cumpleaños Feliz* – 'Happy Birthday' to Pete, was sung with gusto by Spanish, Welsh and English alike. There was no need for a committee meeting or a vote, every member of the choir was unanimous in saying they had had a night to remember.

To this day Pete informs people back in Wales that he spent his 40th birthday in an old people's home. He thoroughly enjoyed the *Residencia* experience, as did one of the younger choristers who was last seen being dragged into a cupboard by Miss Torrevieja 1956!

*

On another occasion, we had arranged for a mixed voice choir to perform at the impressive Benidorm City Hall. Joining our choristers was a visiting choir from Murcia and also Benidorm's top choir. For the concert's finale, the choirs had agreed to perform together 'Speed Your Journey', from Verdi's *Nabucco*. At almost the last minute, the accompanists and the musical directors of the Spanish choirs became uncertain about playing such a prestigious piece on the piano. Down-to-earth Joan, our musical director responded with a statement along the lines of, "Stuff and nonsense. If they won't play it, I will." So it was that Joan and I went to the final rehearsals of the Spanish choirs in downtown Benidorm.

On our way to meet the choir, Joan was unusually nervous, perhaps worried about the language problems. She also wondered if she could succeed in gelling two choirs into one, when they spoke a language she didn't understand. We arrived at the venue and opened the door to the rehearsal room. The view that greeted us was both formal and daunting. The choirs, plus a delegation of officials from the two choirs, were sitting waiting for Joan. Sensing Joan was still nervous,

I went ahead to make the introductions. The next second I felt a swift breeze whizz past me as Joan overtook me at the speed of light. Joan won't mind me telling you that she was over 70 years of age at this time. She grabbed the first man she reached and, as is the custom in Spain, kissed him on each cheek. Joan then announced to her new Spanish friend in perfect English that she was delighted to meet him and was looking forward to working with his choir.

At this point I felt it important to point out to Joan that the gentleman she had accosted was in fact the caretaker of the building, and that the people she needed to speak to were standing patiently just to one side. They each looked slightly bemused, but by the time I made the introductions, Joan was in full flow. Deciding my presence was totally unnecessary, I exited stage right and sat in the bar next door with a newspaper and a cool beer. Anticipating a long wait and calculating that I would get through at least another two drinks, I was surprised to see Joan enter the bar 20 minutes after I had left her with the choristers. She told me everything was fine and asked me to get her a Martini. Indeed, everything was fine, and the concert was superb with the joint item provoking a standing ovation.

After the concert we were amazed to discover that the local choir had planned a meal for us. They assured us that the food was 'nothing special' but when we saw the feast laid out, with steak, salmon, pork and trout, accompanied by the best red and white wines, we realised that 'nothing special' qualified for the understatement of the century. We stayed as long as was possible, but were unable to enjoy what had been prepared. Our buses had been booked for midnight and, although not exactly turning into pumpkins, the extra cost incurred by going beyond midnight might have turned the choir treasurer prematurely grey! So, after filling our boots as quickly as was decent, we sadly had to leave. If we left any later then we would have to pay an extra day's coach hire, and besides, there was a rather special announcement to make back at the hotel.

Later that night, or actually just after midnight, I felt privileged to ask the choir chairman if he would announce to the choir that Joan had been awarded the MBE in the Queen's Birthday Honours List. Until that moment, other than Joan, I was the only person present who was aware of the honour and, like Joan, I was sworn to secrecy. I had to know because at the stroke of midnight, I was to be telephoned with the news of Joan's MBE and could then make the announcement.

In addition to her services to music, years earlier Joan had formed the Cancer Challenge Singers who helped her raise thousands of pounds for the Cancer Challenge charity which she was instrumental in founding. The honour was richly deserved but I couldn't resist suggesting to the assembled choir that MBE might have stood for 'Mrs Big 'Ead'. In reality, nothing could be further from the truth. Her son butted in saying that I should not be so disrespectful to his mother, adding that MBE actually stood for 'Mam Big 'Ead'.

*

While many of the fabulous concerts given by touring Welsh choirs to packed concert halls or churches have developed out of months of painstaking rehearsal, as we have already seen, choirs also have a great reputation for impromptu performances. On some occasions they become renowned for talents other than singing, and some of the afterglow 'routines' are actually well rehearsed.

After one evening concert the local mayor invited all 130 members of our visiting choir and wives to a party in the park. He telephoned his brother who ran the park's kiosk and bar and, a couple of hours later, the result was a huge and noisy 'conga' of two choirs, plus friends, snaking their way around the park.

Offering a free bar to thirsty choristers contributed to the mayor losing his seat at the next election. This was partly because our happy band of Welsh tourists partied their way through 50 per cent of the town's annual entertainment budget. The opposition parties couldn't wait to bury his political career when news leaked out of his generosity to the *extranjeros* (foreigners).

The afterglow is another example of extempore singing bursting out after the stress, albeit enjoyable stress, of a concert, when choristers and their supporters can relax in a bar. Many choirs believe they have the best afterglow in Wales, and I am certainly not going to choose, but one which springs to mind, happened in a remote Spanish town. It was famous for the manufacture of a certain type of rope, plus its magnificent medieval cathedral. On first entering the sacred building it appeared a dark, almost intimidating, place, but it boasted the most fantastic acoustics, which brought the best out of all performing choirs. The town hierarchy, delighted that our choir had performed in a charity concert in their cathedral and anticipating the ensuing good publicity, arranged to take over a bar and put out tables in the street.

The snacks were consumed, the beer and wine flowed and the choir, town mayor, town councillors and their partners were all enjoying the evening. Then the singing started. At first the music went along the traditional Welsh lines, with 'Calon Lân' and 'Men of Harlech' being well received. At this point the local police decided to follow the sound of singing and investigate. The police were soon sent packing by the town mayor. The mayor of a Spanish town is a powerful and influential figure. Impressed by the way the mayor had handled the police, a concert party from the choir decided to reward him with their version of the Baloo the Bear / King Louie scene from the *Jungle Book*. Entering into the spirit of the musical film, they sang, they danced and when they felt it was necessary, even swung from the surrounding trees. When this 'entertainment' started, some of us were in a nearby bar watching Real Madrid beat Manchester United in a Champions League match. We were encouraged to leave the bar to see what was happening in the Welsh version of *Jungle Book*.

As we watched the tree swinging and dancing, I looked across to see how the mayor and his party were responding. Although completely bemused by what was happening, they smiled politely and occasionally laughed in the right places. Such was the wonderful atmosphere generated by the whole occasion, we thought we might get away with any perceived breach of protocol. That belief disappeared when, to my horror, the orangutan, King Louie, sat on the lap of the mayor, while his partner in crime, Baloo the Bear, sat on the lap of the deputy mayor. King Louie then proceeded to do what monkeys sometimes do. He stuck a finger in the ear of the mayor and another to the nostril. Having first offered Baloo the opportunity to share, King Louie then appeared to eat the contents. While all this was happening several choristers were playing their part by serenading the local dignitaries whilst swinging from the surrounding trees.

The evening ended soon afterwards!

*

Another choir's afterglow came to an abrupt end in Spain, although on this occasion the choristers, unlike the last choir, had done nothing to damage international relationships. It was the end of the tour and, after their successful concert, members of the male voice choir retired to enjoy the local bar's hospitality. Carlos, the bar owner, had organized a barbecue and, as the bar was fairly crowded, our boys decided to take their drinks outside and sing near the barbecue. By this stage drinks were being downed at the rate of knots, when suddenly the heavens opened. Our Welsh Valleys boys were determined to sing in the rain. After all, coming from where they did, they were well used to the wet stuff falling from the sky. What they didn't realise was that when it rains on the Costas, it really rains. Cats and dogs come nowhere near capturing the intensity of Spanish rain. In no time at all, the terrace was flooded, yet the boys continued to sing. Despite their fantastic resolve, their spirits were soon dampened both in glass and mind. The canopy under which they sheltered, now full of water, collapsed. Much to the amusement of the rest of the choir, it only drenched the tenors.

The horrified landlord, eager to make up for the soaking, offered free drinks all round. The tenor section, although pleased at the offer, was also slightly miffed. They suggested that the free drinks should be given only to their section of the choir. After all, it was they who had earned the free drink. That suggestion was rejected by a somewhat inebriated musical director who was called upon to give a ruling. So, in the end, dry and soaking choristers all enjoyed the landlord's free drink. It was to everyone's good fortune that the concerts had been completed before this particular evening. The combination of alcohol and a good drenching had overnight turned the choir into a quartet, as the great majority reached for the throat lozenges and hangover cures.

*

Another touring Welsh choir had their performance affected by the problems water can pose. At the end of a great week we organized a farewell evening concert at the hotel. Everything was arranged with the hotel manager and the choir's stage manager, well ahead of the concert. The choir would sing from the terrace near the huge outdoor swimming pool. With everything organized, what could go wrong?

We retired to a local beach with some friends to enjoy a lunch of fresh sardines, downed with the help of a few beers.

That was followed by a siesta on the sand and, my job done, the feeling that there is no better way to prepare for an evening concert. We left the beach in plenty of time and, after a shave and shower, I went down to the bar for a swift drink, before the concert started.

As I went outside I was stopped in my tracks. What was going on? The audience was sitting where the choir should have been standing. There were hundreds of people, but no singers. Where was the choir?

The hotel manager explained. It seems that in our absence the choristers had decided to sing from the concrete island in the middle of the pool. There was no disputing the fact that the setting was fantastic and the lighting spectacular. The only problem was that with 40 metres of water between the choristers and the nearest member of the audience, no-one could hear the choir.

It took some time and a lot of shouting from Big Billy, the choir stage manager and very big bloke, plus a very patient audience, before we eventually managed to move everything and everyone, and a shortened version of the concert started 30 minutes late.

Some members of the audience had taken advantage of the lull in the proceedings to top-up at the bar. These included those who had arrived expecting to see the hotel's usual entertainment bill of 'pass the orange', bingo and a slightly blue comedian. They became loud and not even Big Billy could keep them quiet. Neither could the comedian who had decided to come along anyway, to watch the concert with his magician friend Marvo and his glamorous 'female' assistant Derrick the drag artist. Well, Derrick was from Cwmtwrch. They had all come to see the choir.

Order was restored and eventually it turned out to be a great off-the-cuff evening. The night was made even better when Pete, one of the young top tenors, won the hotel's Miss Swimming Costume competition.

As Pete was a single boy living with his Mam and sharing a room on tour with Bleddyn, a bottom bass, the boys did wonder where he found his very fetching costume.

The following day, determined to perform from the island in the pool, several of the choristers and their intrepid conductor, swam, paddled and waded their way to their new performance space. It was all a trifle incongruous as they stood there in assorted swimwear singing, 'The Rhythm of Life' and 'The Rose'. They then rounded off the concert with a rousing rendition of 'Calon Lân' and the Welsh national anthem. Once again, very few could hear them, except for their wives, friends and several waiters who stood in the pool and cheered and applauded wildly. We still can't decide whether the enthusiastic response was a result of fine singing or whether the entertainment was actually provided by the rich assortment of bathers, Speedos, bulging bellies and bandages.

*

Two wonderful characters were Dilys and Delyth, who were quickly christened the Dedoreth Twins. They constantly encountered trouble with those new fangled apparatus called lifts. They always appeared on the wrong floor, usually with a harassed and sweaty Spanish youngster. Dilys and Delyth were actually staying on the fifth floor, but always seemed to end up on the ninth even when they were aiming for the ground floor. They would enter on the fifth but by the time they had ceased talking long enough to press the button for the ground floor, elsewhere in the building, someone had called the lift to the eighth or ninth floor. Thinking they'd arrived at ground level Dilys and Delyth would vacate the lift, only to discover that they were in fact on the eighth floor. Of course, by the time they realised their mistake someone else in the building had called the lift, so they pressed for it and repeated the process, this time getting out on the fifth floor. And so it went on... and up... and down... and on and on...

It is interesting that when stories circulate amongst choristers about characters many of them are related to the weather and relationships. Brendan was a chorister, recently divorced. He was determined to go back to Wales with a fantastic suntan as he was convinced it would help him 'pull a bird'. Despite these good intentions, after each concert he would allow the large brandies to take their toll, so he was never up in time the next day to catch any sun. Towards the end of his trip, rummaging through the cupboards in his apartment, Brendan found an old bottle of fake tan which had been left by previous occupants. Thinking of the girls he would pull back home and determined to return with a tan, he plastered himself with what was clearly, though not to him, outdated tanning lotion. All he succeeded in doing was to turn the palms of his hands bright orange.

Back at home in Wales, Brendan worked at a bank. He now had the added problem of how to count people's money in the bank. He couldn't really wear gloves in June, so he took an extra week off work and waited for the tan to disappear.

*

Geraint and Anne enjoyed everything about their trips to Spain, everything that is except for the tea. "Can't get a good cuppa char on the Costas," lamented Anne. Each year they'd visit the Costas and each trip Anne would pack a case full of teabags and a kettle. The choir trip was no different.

A late afternoon arrival at the choir's hotel meant that several hours had passed since Anne had her last cup of tea. Nerves were frayed. Eventually they had their room key and as soon as they were in the room Anne set about making her favourite drink. Unpacking could wait. Tea bags and a recently repaired kettle were rescued from the suitcase, along with an adapter for the kettle plug. Because they were seasoned travelers, Anne and Geraint had brought digestive biscuits and packets of Kit Kat from Abdul's Spar on the corner of their Valleys street. Excitedly, she opened the biscuits and switched on the kettle. Help! For some reason the kettle wasn't warming. Neither were the lights working. Had 60 Welsh people all wanting a cup of tea caused an overload to the system?

Having failed to locate a master switch, Geraint went down to reception where he found the rest of the party complaining about the same thing. Well, most were complaining. The single blokes were in the bar sampling a pint of tea substitute. Unpacking could wait.

No tea, no shower, what a shambles! The hotel maintenance department failed to locate the problem, so a couple of noisy generators were installed as a temporary measure. The noise from the generators was unbearable and not actually solving the problem.

"Never mind, all muck in, and it's off to the bar on the corner."

Although still no sign of tea, Anne was starting to enjoy the coffee, which Geraint had liberally laced with brandy. All was almost well with the world when the receptionist arrived and told the group that the electrics problem at the hotel had been solved. To apologise for the inconvenience he also informed the group that if they'd care to visit the hotel bar he'd organise a free drink for the party. Sangria all round!

On reflection, as Geraint and Anne retired to their room, the day hadn't seemed so bad after all. The free drinks and the brandy-laced coffee had kicked in and the sun would be shining tomorrow and no concert until the evening. Time for a cuppa before bed.

"Stick the kettle on," said Geraint, "I'll have a quick shower and join you for a cuppa." (Note, not a quick cuppa and join you for a shower. I suppose they had been married a long time.)

With the sound of Geraint singing 'Bread of Heaven' in the shower, everything seemed to be working just fine. The cup of tea would be well worth waiting for thought Anne as she triumphantly plugged in her kettle... Ffuumph. Blackout, followed by a yell and a curse from the bathroom as, by now stumbling about in the darkness, the naked and wet Geraint had cracked his shin against that little sink. "You know the one, bidet it's called, the little sink you wash your smalls in."

*

Gwyn, accompanied by his wife, Delyth, and his male voice choir, arrived at their destination. They were all excited by the lovely new hotel into which they were booked. Everyone was looking forward to the welcome party in the bar. The choristers dispersed to their rooms for a quick change of clothing and a spot of unpacking. Gwyn had decided that once they reached their room there would be time for a swift one from the duty free whisky he'd bought and Del could have her duty free Baileys. Soon all would be well with the world. They arrived at their room, placed the new-fangled key card into the lock and hey presto, the green light flashed and in they went.

'But hey, the lights don't work and I can't switch the TV on," said Delyth, who was looking forward to the Spanish version of *Eldorado*.

Gwyn set off to complain to reception where he was greeted by the sight of several choristers equally intent on complaining. Were they all looking forward to *Eldorado*? The long-suffering staff on reception pointed out that in order for the lights and everything else to work, customers must place the key card into the box located just inside the door of the hotel room. "Bloody clever, eh?" thought Gwyn as he returned to the room.

The reception staff thought they might check to see if their new and much valued guests were coping. I was told that as they walked along the corridor the sound the staff heard from the rooms was one of clinking glasses and hearty laughter. Surely *Eldorado* wasn't that funny? The residents of each room were no doubt laughing at their own confusion over the key cards.

*

We had organized a charity concert at one of the new style senior persons' residences. Basically these are up-market, timeshare apartment complexes, for wealthy over 60s from around Europe. The concert was organized here because although the residence was obviously all about selling their timeshare, the owners did a lot of good in the local community and the concert was to be a charity event. They also promised to look after the choir and wives with a few drinks and a buffet after the concert. Of course, the owners also wanted to offer a short presentation to their 'elderly' visitors from the UK.

Armed with a glass of bubbly, a quickish tour around the complex was followed by a short film and a brief question and answer session before the group got themselves ready for the concert.

The question and answer session ended somewhat sooner than our hosts had hoped when Brenda, the ageing mother-in-law of bottom bass Terry, obviously referring to the property on offer, but perhaps with one eye on Roland, the immaculately turned out Swiss sales manager, innocently asked "Do they come with erection and will we get felt..." There was obviously a lot more of this question to come, but Brenda got cut off in mid query by a group of choristers creased with laughter.

A successful concert and afterglow followed. Lots of money was raised for worthy causes in the area but, strangely, Roland was nowhere to be seen.

*

Affectionately known as 'Aussie John', John obviously suffered from a crisis of identity. John was born and raised in Melbourne Australia, lived in Spain with his English wife Bernice, and was a passionate supporter of Welsh rugby. He was a great supporter of our concerts in Spain and even the occasional concert in Wales. In fact John loved almost all things Welsh, including my partner Jennifer, but could be very opinionated. This was proved when he turned up on our doorstep, barged into the kitchen and proceeded to try and teach Jennifer how to make cawl. That didn't go down too well – John's opinion, that is, not the cawl. Whenever we had a Welsh choir in Torrevieja, John would distribute posters around the local bars, a tough job, but someone had to do it. He religiously attended most concerts and every afterglow. At this time John had recently been registered blind and he attended a specialist unit at the hospital in Alicante. The experts there decided that it was worth operating on him because the chances of success were good and if successful, the operation would offer John and Bernice, by now in their 60s, a much better quality of life. John had the operation in the summer and by the time we arrived in Torrevieja with our next choir, John's eyesight was gradually improving but he still wore dark glasses and most things were a bit of a blur. This was the case whether or not he'd had a drink!

On this particular concert tour we had taken Craig and his beautiful girlfriend Leah to Spain to support the choir. At about 16 years of age, both Craig and Leah were champion Welsh dancers and we thought this would make a nice contrast to a male voice choir concert. It was a wonderful concert evening, played out on a stage with a wooden floor, perfect to accentuate the sound of Craig and Leah's clogs. We had reserved seats in the front row for John and Bernice and they duly took them at the start of the concert.

I am sure the choir wouldn't mind me saying that, as good as they were, the biggest cheer of the night was for the 'Dawns y Glocsen'. This is a clog dance which contains a section where the dancer extinguishes a lit candle with his clogs. The candle is placed in the top of a bottle, appropriately in this case, an empty Rioja bottle. The musicians play, the dancers dance and at some stage in the dance the lead male dancer leaps in the air and extinguishes the flame with his feet. When Craig extinguished the flame the audience roared their approval.

After the concert we retired to the bar and were joined at our table by Aussie John and Bernice. John went on to explain that although some days he felt comfortable with the improvement in his eyesight since the operation, it was only when he saw the flame of the candle and Craig putting it out that he realised his eyesight was indeed getting much better. Well, his eyesight might have been improving, the same couldn't be said for those at our table. There was not a dry eye to be seen. We were all misty eyed and emotional at John's news. Gracious as ever, we all accepted John's offer of a round of drinks, even if we had to get them ourselves.

*

During one of our visits to the Costa del Sol, CF Malaga played Real Betis in the Spanish La Liga, a game which is almost a local derby match. Thirty one thousand and thirteen packed into *Estadio La Rosaleda*. That is 31,000 Spaniards, mostly supporting Malaga, plus me, our driver and eleven members of the visiting Welsh male voice choir whom I had persuaded to come to the match. The first 30 minutes passed rather uneventfully and it was then that I learnt a new Spanish word. I had wondered why the vast majority of the crowd seemed to be dressed for winter when we 13 Brits stood at the back of the terrace, an open terrace without a roof, wearing T-shirts, shorts and flip flops. It was about this time that the heavens opened and, as if by magic, every Spanish person around us seemed to be wearing rain jackets or plastic macs. In addition, every one of them seemed to possess a *paraguas*, an umbrella, my new Spanish word.

What should we do? We were getting soaked, but it was warm rain. Although we had little interest in the match, we were enjoying the atmosphere which would no doubt soon be enhanced by a few beers and a song or two. Although our driver was with us, our hired minibus was some distance away. Let's stay and enjoy the game, the beer, the occasion. Despite our decision, we could hardly be accused of blending in with the surroundings. Malaga wore blue and white, Betis green and white and, as is the want of most Welsh on tour, our soaking T-shirts were red. I think the locals enjoyed our presence in their midst, even if it only confirmed their opinion of daft foreigners on the Costas.

*

We have already met the late Gerald and it is now time to be introduced to the late Dai, a chorister who arranged his own funeral, in advance of his death.

He had left instructions that the car taking him to his own funeral would drive around for ten minutes so that he really could be late for his own funeral service. Such was his tardiness in life, his mates at the choir had always told him, "Dai, you will be late for your own funeral," so he made sure he was.

Dai had also left money and instructions at the local social club so that everyone could have a drink on Dai. However, on arrival at the club, mourners were greeted by a note on the door which read: "In honour of our dearly departed friend, THE LATE Dai, who has left money to buy everyone a drink, the club will open ten minutes later than indicated in the funeral service notes."

Despite suffering a long illness, Dai had battled on and kept his Welsh Valley sense of humour intact throughout his life and beyond.

*

When running a tour or trying to manage a choir, timekeeping is vitally important. I know of one choir who has invented a novel way of tackling the problem. When on tour they insist on the buses leaving at midnight after each concert and afterglow. That way, the boys don't get confused. Let's hope they adjust their watches when arriving in a new country.

Rather like the iconic *Grand Slam*, the boys were in Paris for the match. The rugby club choir was enjoying an evening stroll along the Pigalle. Anne, the attractive young accompanist, was attracting her fair share of attention from the locals, none of whom seemed to want her to play the piano. Of course, the choristers split into two camps. The one that was over-protective of the lovely Anne, despite the fact she was more than capable of looking after herself and the other camp who thought it was a bit of a laugh to play along with the locals in their bids for Anne's em 'services'. Of course, no money changed hands. Anne was always safe in the choir family.

As the night progressed, some of the boys decided to wander off in search of some action. They found a likely bar and returned to the meeting point to tell the other boys about this fantastic place. However, on their return to the original bar there was no sign of the boys and more worryingly no sign of Anne. The barman told them that he thought their friends and the pretty mademoiselle had returned to the hotel. The boys, obviously concerned that Anne might be sold into slavery, decided to check out one last place: the one down the lane. "The one with the girls inviting us in. The bar with the flashing neon lights."

A dozen or so of the boys went on ahead and duly got in. Unfortunately, the rest of the guys were not so lucky. The bouncers wouldn't allow them entry. It seems that a number of Welsh choristers had turned up and were drinking and singing the night away. This didn't sit too well with the girls of the bar who were being completely ignored. A few words were exchanged and the odd scuffle had broken out. There was no major problem and the singing continued and, somewhat mysteriously, the boys swore they could hear a piano.

How to get in? The bouncers were having none of it and had moved inside the club locking the heavy door behind them. Occasionally they would open the small grill on the door to say that the bar was full and nobody was coming in. Then, a moment of inspiration, Alun, veteran second XV prop forward and bottom bass, removed his bobble hat, teeth and glasses, combed what was left of his hair and banged on the grill. The grill opened and Alun, in his best French and placing his blood donor card to the grill, shouted *"Gendarme, Pays de Galle. Gendarme,* Police, Wales Police!" Seeing his makeshift police ID, the bouncers opened the door and let Alun in with his police colleagues. Perhaps this was an occasion where shouting loudly and gesticulating wildly equates to a reasonable grasp of a foreign language.

Unfortunately, as word of the 'police's' arrival reached the bar, everyone else legged it through the back door. The escapees apparently included several members of a Welsh choir accompanied by a very pretty girl who played the piano. Alun replaced his teeth, sat on a bar stool and enjoyed a few drinks with his butties, and his new friends at the club. "Special discount, for Welsh police, mind you."

By the way, the first time Selwyn was seen without his French beret on his head, was when he removed it to make a collection for the driver. The choir was flying home at the time!

CHAPTER 6

What the Average Male Voice Chorister Knows about Women

CHAPTER 7

Choir Practice

❝IT'S STRANGE. THE more I practise, the luckier, I become."

Was it Gary Player who summed up his golfing life, thus? The sentiment could be applied to any sport and every art form. It is certainly true in the world of male voice choirs in that the choirs that practise the most are often the 'luckiest' in securing good contracts and enjoying competition success.

I am sometimes asked to attend a choir practice, often to address the choir, in order to offer advice and encouragement with regards to undertaking a tour. After that initial introduction we would often meet again so that I can update the choir and hand out tickets, plus finalized itineraries. This is rarely a hardship and presents an opportunity for me to get to know the choir better, usually over a drink following the rehearsal.

I try to arrive a little early and, as I step off the train, I hope that the church hall or practice room is near a pub. Naturally shy, even after all these years, I still find it quite intimidating to stand and speak before a large group. A little Dutch courage has worked for me in the past.

Thankfully, as I arrive at the practice room, suitably relaxed after my diversion to the pub, the first thing I notice is the friendly and welcoming atmosphere. The guys seem to know who I am and are expecting me. More importantly they know why I am there.

My contact at one particular choir is secretary Selwyn, a dapper man with sandy hair and a nice line in Pringle sweaters. He is sitting with treasurer Stan, a larger man. Golf club sweater, and a shock of white hair. Stan and Selwyn are collecting subs and seem to have an inordinate amount of paperwork in front of them. I find out later that Sec' Selwyn and Subs' Stan are affectionately known as the SAS, Selwyn And Stan.

They seem to be the main organisers, along with Peter the chairman. I am left thinking it is just as well he is called Peter and not Oliver. Otherwise, it would be SOS running the show, although a cry for help might yet prove appropriate. Selwyn greets me and introduces me to Stan and Peter ('Please call me Pete'). They explain that with an Eisteddfod on the horizon, Gareth, the musical director, would appreciate a quick run through a few of the pieces before I speak to the choir. During the interval Selwyn would read the notices and then Pete would introduce me.

Gareth is tallish, thirtyish, slim and prematurely balding. He is also from a new school of conductor, with new ideas which don't always sit well with some of the 'old school choristers'. Gareth is keen to take the choir forward and he too greets me warmly. He tells me that touring is good for choir morale and bonding. He thinks they are ready now. This is promising, the musical director is on our side. Gareth introduces me to Andrea, a student who is the choir's deputy accompanist. In another setting to be greeted warmly by Andrea would no doubt be a pleasure too, but I'm thinking chance would be a fine thing. It seems that Rose, the usual accompanist is on holiday. Andrea is Rose's granddaughter. Choirs often keep it in the family. Granddaughter? How old is Rose, I wonder.

Rather unnecessarily, Gareth thanks me for allowing him "first go at this lot". By now the men, approximately 70 in number with an average age not far short of this figure, have organized themselves into sections and are sitting on wooden chairs in four rows. A few throats are cleared as Gareth moves to his music stand and stands before them.

"Good evening, gentlemen, so good of you to turn out on such an inclement evening. Let us hope that we will all be rewarded by some outstanding singing." With that he turns to me, winks and, to hoots of derision from the choir, says "I somehow doubt it".

Before the practice can start new school Gareth takes the choir in a series of breathing exercises. Later in the pub I'm told, "Not so long ago, the only requirement to join this choir was a limp and a cabinet full of tablets. Now before we sing, we have to prove we can breathe!"

Gareth suggests they start with one of the test pieces for the forthcoming Eisteddfod.

"I do hate this piece," says a deep voice from the bottom bass section. A mass rummage for music through assorted briefcases and files and everyone seems ready. All except Bernard.

"Wot's he say? Wot we singing?" It seems Bernard is quite deaf and, not for the first time, he has forgotten his hearing aid.

To me and my, admittedly, uneducated ear, the first piece sounds excellent and as the only 'guest' I am not sure whether to applaud. However, all is not well with Gareth. He asks the tenor section to take it again and, after they have run through the particular part that so offended Gareth the first time round, the choir is asked to sing the piece again. This time Gareth, rather than conduct from his music stand, chooses to walk around the choir, stopping at intervals where his expert ear can pick out which individuals are not hitting the right notes.

The boys are warned that, although better than last week, it is still not good enough and the Eisteddfod judges will mark them down on certain points. Gareth moves on to the next piece, and the next, and the next... then calls for a break and invites Selwyn to make any announcements.

"Subs should be in, tickets and raffle tickets need to be sold for the annual concert. Apologies from Gerry and Mike, their transport seems to have let them down."

It is a worry that Gerry and Mike, two of the younger members of the choir are missing. From the general conversation I discover that they are both paramedics.

"I 'ope I don't fall off my ladder when those two silly buggers are on call," says Wilf, the semi-retired window cleaner.

Apologies are also read out from Dai Bottom Bass, who can't be with us tonight as Aunty Lily needs a lift to Bristol Airport.

"Auntie Lily's good to us," Selwyn reminds the choir.

She is the aunt of Dai Bottom Bass and was left a lot of money when her husband, Dai the Builder, affectionately known to all as Bob, passed away. Lily now supports the choir with the occasional contribution to choir funds. The notices are concluded with a reminder that the choir is due to sing at the funeral of a relative of one of the choristers, young Tom's mother's, cousin's, uncle's elder brother, or something like that. The bus will leave the club at 12.30 next Tuesday. Sandwich and a pint for the choir afterwards, black blazers and choir ties to be worn.

"NO, BERNARD, CHOIR TIES, NOT BLACK TIES."

"Where's your hearing aid Bernard?"

"What's he say?" asks Bernard, to no-one in particular. And now it's my turn.

Selwyn asks Peter to step up and Peter introduces and welcomes me. It seems it is choir protocol that the chairman welcomes outsiders. Peter suggests I might want to join the choir.

"He don't look that daft," shouts a voice from the back row. I take that as a compliment. Unless I am very much mistaken everyone seems to be in remarkably good humour. Let's try not to spoil it.

In an attempt to break the ice, I explain that I will try not to keep them too long because I know how much they enjoy their practice, "and besides Gareth tells me that you need all the practise you can get". This remark is greeted mostly with laughs, accompanied by a few howls of derision aimed at Gareth. I outline our plans and invite questions – not always a good idea. "Speak up," shouts Bernard.

"Do we 'ave to 'ave inoculations to go?" Before I can answer this previously unasked question – Spain is the destination after all – one of the tenors pipes up with, "Not before we go Bill, but depending on 'ow lucky you get, you might need a jab when we get 'ome." Bill is 85 years of age.

"How much is a cup of tea in Spain?"

"What about a piano?"

"If we want to attract an audience, better not use our picture on the publicity," says Frank, a top tenor. "The bottom basses are ugly buggers. They 'ave the perfect faces for radio."

"I am off on tour with the rugby club before we goes to Spain," says Big Al. His cousin, Little Al is also in the choir. At six foot five, Big Al towers over his cousin Little Al, by at least an inch.

"My missus won't know what I look like after two weeks away" says Big Al.

"Don't worry," says Little Al. "Tell her you look like Robert Redford.

"Your missus does like Robert Redford," says his cousin.

Everyone is up for the trip and they promise to have a deposit ready in two weeks. Gareth is worried that they might be a couple of tenors short. In an attempt at humour, I suggest that if they were short of two tenners (tenors) I could lend them twenty quid.

Quick as a flash Brian Bottom Bass hits back with, "Twenty quid for two tenors? You'd be lucky to get £20 for the whole bloody lot of them."

Later, I am told that Brian is a well-balanced Welshman.

"A chip on each shoulder and a pint in each hand." Brian possesses a voice so deep that he made Lee Marvin sound like Aled Jones.

"What's he say?" asked Bernard.

*

It has been my great fortune to work with choirs from all parts of the UK, Europe, Canada and Australia. It is interesting to observe choirs at practice and compare the differences between a Welsh male voice choir and, perhaps, a Spanish choir.

A Spanish Mediterranean choir practice probably wouldn't begin until 10 p.m. What we have to realise is that the siesta is still sacred in most parts of Spain, particularly in the summer months. The Spanish men start work early and stop for lunch and siesta, before starting again at 5 p.m. Many of the choristers are, therefore, unable to get to the practice before 10 p.m.

As with the Welsh choir practice I arrive in plenty of time but, rather than seek out a local bar, I am offered a beer from the bar that fronts the choir practice room and am joined by several members of the choir who are having a few pre-practice drinks as they wait for their working colleagues to arrive.

Ricardo the choir musical director, or maestro, joins us and, as he sips a beer, he complains to the choir about their drinking habits before they practise. It seems he has this conversation with them every week.

At 10.20 p.m. prompt, only 20 minutes late, maestro starts the practice. Tenor Francisco complains that it is too soon to start, as most of the musicians haven't arrived. This choir is accompanied by a mostly youthful string orchestra. Through the next 45 minutes, lutes, mandolins, guitars, choristers and musicians turn up in dribs and drabs.

Ricardo, who formed the choir some 40 years ago and had been awarded a medal by the King of Spain for his services to music, and was very well known in Spain, was getting a little frustrated at his choristers' inability to concentrate on the music. He points me out and tells the choir that I have travelled from Wales for this rehearsal and they are letting me down as well as themselves. This didn't work! Francisco and Manolo, whom I had known for years and with whom my family shared a paella the other night, points out that I was actually staying about one kilometre away and that after the practice they were taking me to a pub! By now Ricardo had had enough. He raises his voice, but only ever so slightly, and tells the choir he would walk away unless they started behaving immediately. The choir had so much respect for Ricardo; they knew they had upset him. From that point on the practice resembled what one would expect at home. When, eventually, all the musicians arrived, they added another dimension to the sound.

It was a wonderful sound and, for me, created a memorable summer's night on the Spanish Mediterranean. Thankfully, one of any number of nights we shared with this group but I can't help thinking how different their seemingly chaotic practice was when compared with the relatively organized practices at home.

Don't ask me to judge which is right and which is wrong. Each to their own.

Joke from the Coach II

An Englishman, Scotsman and Welshman are tendering for a building job with the local council. Each man is to be interviewed for the job by the unlikely named Cllr Selwyn Fiddler, head of planning and the man in charge of the building project.

Henry the English builder is the first to be interviewed. Cllr Fiddler asks for a breakdown of costs and the Englishman's price.

"£3,000," says Henry. "£1,000 labour, £1,000 materials and £1,000 profit."

Hooray, thought Cllr Fiddler. "Hooray," said Henry!

Mac the Scotsman is next in with a quote. It's the same procedure, price, breakdown of costs.

"£6,000," says Mac, the canny Scotsman.

"£2,000 for the best material, £2,000 for the best craftsmen and, aye, there will be £2,000 profit."

Cllr Fiddler thanked Mac and showed him to the door before pouring himself a large glass of whisky. He was savouring the whisky as he contemplated the two quotations when in walked local builder and odd job man of the parish, one Thomas Caradog Jones, otherwise known as 'Breeze Block Jones'.

"Bore da, Selwyn," said Tom, pouring himself a whisky.

"Good morning Tom" said Cllr Fiddler. "Well let's have it but, I warn you, that things is tight and we have two excellent quotations for the job," said Cllr Fiddler, eager to get shot of his near neighbour who was already helping himself to another whisky.

Tom sat at the desk and said, "Well Selwyn, I think we can bring this job in at £9,000."

"What – how much?" spluttered Cllr Fiddler. "You is 'aving a laugh. Could you offer a breakdown, please?"

"Well," said Tom. "That's £3,000 for me and £3,000 for you and we'll give the job to the Englishman! I'm off on tour with the choir."

The following week Cllr Fiddler joined the choir, just in time to join the tour.

(I have changed the names to protect the innocent – the Scotsman's name wasn't Mac!)

CHAPTER 8

Not Just a Choir, More a Way of Life

THE SPANISH LOVE their sport. Football is definitely the most popular, possibly followed by cycling and basketball.

Rugby, although becoming more popular, is some way down the list. However, such is the Welsh passion for rugby, whenever we take a choir to Spain during the round of international matches, we try not to organize a concert which clashes with the rugby. To the Spanish it must all seem rather incongruous as we cram into their bars to watch our national game.

One choir trip coincided with a Wales match against Australia, so we arranged for our large group of about 80 choristers to watch the game at a friend's bar. Fortunately, Bar Carlos was large enough to accommodate our crowd and his normal clientele. We decided to make an afternoon of it, and provided the cosmopolitan bar staff with red T-shirts. On each shirt was printed the words, 'Every day when I wake up, I thank the Lord I'm Welsh'.

Despite our boys again being beaten by a southern hemisphere team, and fairly easily beaten, everyone had a memorable afternoon. Who knows, some of the choristers might even remember a memorable night. Since the earliest tourists took their first tentative steps in a new territory, there have been people hovering around the corner ready to sell them something they patently do not want or need. The Spanish Costas are full of 'looky looky' men. Usually black gentlemen from Senegal, they stride up and down the beach or wander into bars approaching British tourists with the invitation to 'looky looky'. I often wonder how they know we are British. Perhaps it's the way our football or rugby shirts complement our white socks and sandals that gives it away. Or, is it the way our lovingly cultivated beer bellies overhang our Speedos as we compete with the Mediterranean-bronzed Adonis for the attention of the German Frauline or the dusky Spanish señorita? It's uncanny how they do it but the African 'looky looky' men always know which are the Brits!

The 'looky looky' salesmen try to sell tourists fake brand name watches or sunglasses. Belts and jewellery are popular sales items as are dodgy CDs and DVDs. Personally I don't have a problem with 'looky looky' men. In my experience, very few make a nuisance of themselves and generally accept that no means no. At least until next time. I always think these guys are trying to sell you something, rather than try to steal from the unsuspecting foreigner, and one doesn't have to buy.

In my opinion very few tourists are actually fleeced. Indeed many tourists and ex-pats choose to buy from 'looky looky' men and generally know the score. Over the years our team in Spain became friendly with one particular 'looky looky' man, Charlie, to the extent that we would sometimes even take back any watches that had stopped or glasses that had broken. Charlie would change the batteries, fix the glasses and enjoy the occasional Coca Cola with us.

Several days after the aforementioned rugby match in the bar, I bumped into Charlie as he was walking through the town. To my amazement he was wearing one of our specially made T-shirts. I have no idea from whom he got this unique collector's item. What I do know is that our Senegalese friend was proclaiming on his chest, 'Every day when I wake up, I thank the Lord I'm Welsh'. For years afterwards, with his inbred sense of commercialism to the fore, Charlie always sensed when there was a new group of Welsh tourists in the vicinity. You can be sure that whenever he was with them, he would wear his Welsh T-shirt. A clever man Charlie. He must have made a fortune. Mind you, he needed it as rumour had it that he has nine children and two wives to support back in Senegal.

Gethin, a long-standing member of the latest Welsh choir in town, was thrilled with his new Rolex. If, for any reason, he had to move his left arm, he would make sure he did it as theatrically as possible. That way everyone would see his latest acquisition which he bought for just 30 Euros (about £24). He was therefore horrified when one of his choir mates said he'd obviously got it from a 'looky looky' man.

"Why do you say that, butt?" Gethin asked.

"Because it's not genuine," replied his friend.

"How can you tell it's not genuine?"

"Because," said his clever clogs buttie, "Rolex is spelt with an X not CKS".

Your average 'looky looky' man, like his street trader equivalent and the time-share tout, is adept at selling you something you don't particularly want, belt, watch, bracelet, apartment etc., in several languages. The smarter than average chorister can soon get rid of any unwanted attention by speaking a few words of a language completely unknown to all but a select few 'looky looky' men / touts / street traders – Welsh! Even if one doesn't speak the language fluently, we all know a few words which can be regurgitated when confronted by any particular nuisance who asks in several languages where you are from. You might even get away with this when wearing the omnipresent rugby shirt. Your typical Senegalese is not known for their knowledge of Welsh rugby! Reciting the words of a Welsh hymn, or even the national anthem, in a dull monotone voice often works for some.

I accompanied one Welsh choir to Spain and our visit coincided with the start of the 2002 football World Cup, which was co-hosted by Japan and South Korea. The male voice choir, who were in Spain without their wives, settled down for the match between France and Senegal in a local Irish bar.

France, who were the reigning World and European champions, were expected to blow Senegal out of existence, in a footballing sense. Even without their injured captain, the magnificent Zinedine Zidane, the France of Thierry Henry and Marcel Desailly were expected to win easily. As we settled down for the match we were joined in the bar by several 'looky looky' men. For once they were not interested in selling anything and therefore were not laden with items for sale, dodgy or otherwise. They had simply come to watch the game and support their team. I, too, was supporting Senegal. Not usually a betting man, I had placed a small wager on the Africans winning. This was not because I knew too much about the team, but it was based on the fact that there had been several shocks in the first match of a major tournament.

It developed into a bizarre, rather surreal afternoon. The 'looky looky' men grew in excitement and volume, especially when Senegal scored and took a 1–0 lead in the 30th minute with a goal by Papa Bouba Diop, which they protected for the rest of the match. As Senegal caused one of the greatest upsets in the history of World Cup football, it was fascinating to hear the accents of Welsh choristers urging Senegal on. As Welshmen, we have endured more than a few rugby beatings at the hands of Les Bleus, so it was important to support the underdog against France.

There was something bizarre and slightly surreal hearing Welsh choristers with their singsong intonation singing the praises of players who just a few minutes earlier they had never heard of: "There's only one Papa Bouba Diop."

"Give it to El Hadji Diouf, Duw, Duw."

Here we were in an Irish bar in Spain populated with several disgruntled Frenchmen. They were even more disgruntled by the fact that most of the Senegal team played for French clubs. There were also several indifferent Spanish, several Irish who are rarely indifferent to anything, several very happy 'looky looky' Senegalese and a slightly bemused, but very happy Welsh choir. When the final whistle was blown there were great celebrations from some. My excitement at predicting the result and winning my bet disappeared as my bar tab soon took care of any money I would be collecting back home.

In certain parts of the world it is often the case that when something momentous happens in the country the residents of towns and cities take to the streets in their vehicles. The supporters display flags and banners, beep their horns and make as much noise as they can, to celebrate their countrymen's success as they convoy their way through the main highways and byways. Not to be outdone, the Senegalese 'looky looky' men decided their team's momentous victory over France had to be celebrated. They drove their battered old vehicles through the streets, displaying their flags and banners. Bizarrely, each car also seemed to display the Welsh dragon, with most cars containing large Welshmen. The teetotal Senegalese were drunk on the success of their team, while the Welsh were just happy to be in Spain with their new friends!

France were eliminated from the competition without even scoring a goal. Senegal went out at the quarter-final stage, losing 1–0 to Turkey in sudden-death extra time. El Hadji Douf, the African footballer of the year, signed for Liverpool, spat in the faces of several players and one Celtic fan, and went on to become one of the most hated footballers in Britain.

Rejoicing with the Senegalese was not the only time Welsh choristers celebrated some other football team's victory. In Spain, nearly everyone supports one of the two big teams. With the exception of the clubs from the Basque region, such as Athletico Bilbao, Spanish people generally support their local side *and* either Real Madrid or Barcelona. The intensity between the two sets of fans is perhaps more intense even than any British derby, such as the rivalry between Celtic and Rangers or Liverpool and Manchester United, Liverpool and Everton. Perhaps not as intense as the Swansea-Cardiff rivalry, but it is still pretty full on. Indeed most Spanish towns have a supporters' club bar affiliated to either Real or Barca. I will never forget one late night where there were riotous festivities into the next day. Real Madrid had just won their ninth European Cup final and the town where we were staying chose to celebrate the result. The cacophony of sound will always be with me as the raucous noise of car horns beeping merged into the sound of people cheering and chanting at the top of their voices. Youths leapt into the foam-filled fountains of the town, many of their splashes accompanied by the notes of our Welsh male voice choir singing their joy at Real's victory. It could have been anyone's victory. The choristers joined in the fun of the moment, as many of them sang as they stood in the fountain.

It reminds me of the phrase which, I believe, was used by Jeff Stelling of Sky television. Announcing a rare victory by a Welsh football side in Europe and with a smile on his face Mr Stelling announced: "They'll be dancing in the streets of Total Network Solutions tonight." Marvelous stuff, and apologies to the late great Bill Mclaren.

While we bonded with some of the 'looky looky' men from Senegal, we failed to make lasting friendships with certain Moroccans. During an autumn tour of Spain, it became clear that a gang of Moroccan thieves were targeting hotels in the town, including one where our choir was staying. Two of the choristers were naturally annoyed at their rooms being broken into. One of the thieves, however, became over ambitious. In broad daylight he began to rush down the stairs with his stolen haul of goods which worryingly, from a security point of view, included a safe from one of the hotel bedrooms. Either he had given no thought to his escape plan, or else he assumed there would be no-one about at that time of day. He was unlucky in that his speedy descent down the stairs coincided with the more leisurely arrival of members of the Welsh choir who were staying in the hotel. He ran headlong into several large retired gentlemen, most of whom were ex-players of Aber Up and Under RFC.

Returning from a rather boozy choir boat trip, our ex-players and current choristers were definitely in the mood for a spot of crime prevention. Old second row Dai decked the thief with what might best be described as a high tackle, an art Dai had mastered during his playing days. Ex-prop Phil sat on the thief until the police arrived.

On arrival the police helped Phil to his feet, "dodgy knees and hip replacement, see." As the police arrested the miscreant, and not wishing to miss out on the action, Glyndŵr, a sprightly 71-year-old ex-outside half, delivered a swift and powerful kick – a drop kick perhaps – to the robber's arse. "Bravo!" the police applauded.

A Town Mourns

It is inevitable that after so many choir trips, one grows close not just to the members of choirs but also to some of the natives. Cecilio was a great friend to me and my colleague Graham in Torrevieja and, indeed, to all the choirs who visited that part of Spain. One Sunday he travelled 60 miles to meet his family for lunch and, liking a drink, rather than drive, decided to take the bus. Waiting for the return bus outside the *Guardia Civil* barracks, Cecilio was tragically murdered by a bomb planted in the bus stop by ETA. In addition to his death, a young girl was also murdered. Perhaps the only consolation from a horrendous situation was the fact that he spent his last moments with his beloved family.

I believe Cecilio had once been a talented singer until he developed throat cancer. Subsequent operations curtailed his singing career but, as a wonderful musician, Cecilio began to teach the town's youth to play the guitar, lute, mandolin, banjo and all manner of stringed instruments. He formed and conducted the string orchestra who accompanied *Coro y Orquesta Salinas de Torrevieja*. This was the choir (who we met in an earlier chapter) who thought kilts were worn by the Welsh. A short man, with a bald head, huge beard and bigger heart, the whole town turned out for his funeral. We felt honoured to be invited into the church where his choir and orchestra performed during the service. The town square in front of the church was packed with thousands of weeping people. From the reactions of the congregation and the choir, it was clear that it was one of the most emotional days of their lives. It was also the same for me.

One of my, sadly, unfulfilled ambitions was to take Cecilio for a full English breakfast. As a proud Spaniard, he fervently believed that unless something was Spanish, it wasn't any good. As far as he was concerned, everything about Spain was better than anything about anywhere else. Clearly a true patriot.

The proliferation of English pubs, Irish bars, and Chinese restaurants on his beloved Costa Blanca was against everything he held dear. On one occasion, when we invited Cecilio to dine with us at a Chinese restaurant, he surprisingly agreed to join us but decided on arrival that he'd wait for us in the Spanish bar across the road. Good shout actually. Cecilio would often take Graham and I for a Spanish breakfast in his workingman's club and if we ordered something that damaged his Spanish sensibilities, which was often, he would introduce us, in Spanish of course, as his "stupid foreign friends" – and we loved him for it.

When he visited Wales with his choir and orchestra he regularly complained about the poor measures of whisky served in UK pubs. He would study the measure in his glass and with a derisory look on his face, suggest that someone must have spat into the glass as he certainly couldn't see any whisky in it.

On a trip to the Houses of Parliament Graham and I decided that as we had been in the great building on several occasions, we would leave the Spanish to enjoy the tour on their own. Safe in the knowledge that our Spanish friends were being well looked after, we decided to retire to a nearby pub for a quiet and relaxing drink. No sooner had Graham and I arrived in the bar than Cecilio walked in with our friends Francisco and Manolo. Without us realising, they had followed us and were determined that they were not going to the Houses of Parliament when their 'stupid foreign friends' were heading for the pub. It didn't occur to them that on this occasion, at least, they were the foreigners!

In fact they didn't use the word 'pub' but said instead they had tracked us down in order to 'apintiando', a word they had invented, which they assured us meant 'to take a pint'.

Whenever we were in Spain with Cecilio, despite his tongue in cheek critique of his foreign friends, he was always a great friend to our choirs, to me and my family and friends. If you had a problem, call Cecilio. On one occasion when it was unusually rainy and the free day on the beach had to be cancelled for our group of young dancers, singers and musicians, Cecilio, at ten minutes' notice, somehow conjured up a bus – well once he had worked out how to use my mobile phone, he conjured up a bus – and took the whole group on a tour of the area before dropping them off at the beach once the rain had ceased. He was visibly touched when, led by Jennifer, the whole bus started to sing the Simon and

Garfunkel song 'Cecilia, you're breaking my heart', of course adapting it to 'Cecilio, you're breaking my heart'. The man is truly missed.

A great friend and colleague of Cecilio's, and of ours, was the composer Ricardo Lafuente. Affectionately christened Dicky Fountain by some Welsh choristers Ricardo, now sadly deceased, was a famous award-winning composer of *Habaneras* music and the maestro of *Coro y Orquesta Salinas de Torrevieja*. A lovely, humble man, who is missed by all those fortunate enough to know him. As mentioned elsewhere it was our privilege to organize his choir's first visit to the UK. The trip included several days in Wales and a few at the end of the trip in London.

Part of the London section of the tour included a sightseeing bus and walking tour of London. This was organized by a couple of friends from the Metropolitan Police. It enabled us to see a few things and take the occasional short cut not necessarily known to the general public.

Ricardo, on his first trip to the UK, was determined to personally film everything. Such was his enthusiasm for this particular task that we christened him 'Ricky Spielberg'. The joke was that we felt we'd have to surgically remove his camera before he could conduct the choir and orchestra.

By now well into his 60s, this was Ricardo's first visit to the UK and he was struggling with the language and particularly with the traffic driving on the wrong side of the road. His confusion with the direction of the traffic, coupled with his reluctance to remove his video camera from his eye, meant that Ricardo was an accident waiting to happen. The walking part of the London tour was particularly fraught. On one occasion at the exact moment our group disappeared around a corner, a short cut known only to our police guides, I was distracted by a screech of brakes. I turned around just in time to see a London bus stop yards from Ricardo who, camera to face, was heading across the road looking in the opposite direction to both the oncoming traffic and the direction in which his choir was being led. What should I do? Follow the police guides, who were the only people who knew exactly where we were going, or attempt to rescue Ricardo? He had somehow negotiated the London traffic and was now on the other side of the road, seemingly determined to film the red London double-decker bus and its charming driver who was, obviously in a gesture of 'welcome to my city', still waving his fist at the smiling Ricardo. Fortunately Ricardo couldn't understand a word of English.

Obviously I couldn't leave the maestro, so having eventually crossed the busy road, much more slowly than Ricardo, I finally caught up with him. But, by now I had absolutely no idea where the rest of the group were. There was nothing for it but to grab a taxi and, via the sights of Trafalgar Square, Pall Mall and other tourist sites, take Ricardo to where I knew we were to meet the bus. Throughout the taxi ride Ricardo, still with camera to face, was giving a commentary, interspersed by the friendly taxi driver's own comments. In my best, limited Spanish, I explained that the driver had said that black London cabs were probably the most famous in the world. More by luck than judgement, we eventually caught up with the rest of the group who, of course, hadn't even noticed we were missing.

The upshot of 'Ricky Spielberg's' filming was that it formed part of a documentary fly-on-the-wall-style programme produced by the choir's local TV company in Spain. The taxi ride and the bus driver were both remembered with some affection. Sitting before the cameras in the TV studio, Ricardo even quoted me as saying that his taxi was the most famous in the world. He also thanked me for organizing this private excursion for him at no extra cost!

In the years that followed we became close friends and whenever his choir performed at a concert with a UK choir,

Ricardo, aka Dicky Fountain, who never did speak a word of English, would introduce the concert with "Bore da" and often end it with "Nos da", regardless of the time of day and the nationality of the choir. He'd also throw in the occasional "Diolch yn Fawr". He was a lovely, fantastic man.

*

I suppose guides are a little like the RAC or AA men, you trust them and rely on them. Like the guides in British cathedrals who troll through the ancient sites with their umbrellas held aloft, you follow them and hang on their every word.

On one occasion our guide didn't quite live up to the 'follow the umbrella' code of practice. Called to deal with a crisis, she rescued a female chorister who had managed to lock herself in one of the salubrious toilets at the Casino Cultural. Relieved to have been of service to our chorister, she then realised that she needed to relieve herself. Whether the need to use the toilet was heightened by the tension of successfully releasing the chorister, we will never know. What we do know, however, is that she then managed to lock herself in the same toilet. The grateful chorister had left the scene and the guide now had the problem of raising the alarm when there was no-one else in the toilet area, and she also discovered there was no signal on her mobile phone. She somehow managed to attract the attention of another of our guides who was having a quiet beer whilst waiting for his colleague to return from the ladies' toilets. Eventually he managed to rescue her and they both escaped the building. Such was the trauma they had endured, and giggling like children, they decided they needed a cold beer, or two, to recover their composure. Neither of them were seasoned drinkers, so it took them longer than anticipated to recover their composure. Once they had arrived at their alcohol-induced recovery, I received a telephone call from the manager of the Tourist Information

Office, enquiring where I was (my phone had a signal). I told him I was at the Monument to the Choirs with my group of Welsh choristers and asked why he wanted to know my whereabouts. "Because your two guides are sitting in front of me and they have absolutely no idea where their choir is."

When tours are undertaken it is not just the locals who strike you as being characters. That role is often played by members of the choir and on some occasions it is filled by people you would least expect. One night on tour, the accompanist Siân, a lovely 'butter wouldn't melt in her mouth' Welsh girl from the Valleys, stunned everyone by telling a filthy joke. The main ingredient of the joke was an elephant, but it also involved missionaries and their favourite position, foreplay, and what fire and brimstone preachers would call fornication. Word soon spread amongst the choir that Sian had told this joke. At the final concert of the tour, as she started to play the introduction to the 'Rhythm of Life', my colleague Graham marched down the aisle and placed a large china elephant on top of the baby grand piano. Siân collapsed into a fit of giggles. The choir, most of whom were in on the joke, roared with laughter. Until Siân was able to pull herself together, the first verse of 'Rhythm of Life' was performed unaccompanied, not the best way for that particular song to be performed. I felt sorry for the compere who had the task of explaining to the audience, in two languages, what was happening. To be perfectly honest I cannot remember the joke and unfortunately I have lost touch with Siân.

Many choirs produce their own CDs and often take them on tour in order to sell them to members of the audience. Some sell more than others. It has often struck me that more CDs would be sold if the person selling them didn't insist on boring the potential purchaser with a lengthy technical insight into how and where the disc was produced. Beards have grown, finger nails lengthened and I have seen people in the queue lose the will to live as Clive Compact Disc, delivers his extensive lecture on the history of the genesis and evolution of his choir's CD.

In addition to producing their own discs, choirs are also rightly proud of any trophies they have won. A particularly grand and well-organized choir invited me to join them for a photo shoot. I proudly stood with them outside the local rugby club as the photographer snapped away. Positioned in front of the choir was a wonderful array of trophies, shields and various awards.

As I stood shoulder to shoulder with the choristers, I began to realise that I had read their CV and various press releases on many occasions. From the information I had read I could not recall them being such a successful choir. Once the photographer had finished and the choir members started to disperse, I went to the front to look at their many trophies. On closer inspection, I discovered they were for snooker, darts and pool and had clearly been borrowed from the rugby club.

CHAPTER 9

Sinning with the Choir

IT IS AMAZING how many funeral directors, undertakers and the like, are choir musical directors and/or accompanists. Perhaps it is even more amazing that whilst on tour most of them seem to do their utmost to disprove the image of dour, boring men dressed in black.

Having attended many funerals and witnessed these men in their work environment, you can imagine it always comes as a surprise to see them 'at play'. Witnessing, or perhaps it's more accurate to say listening to, funeral director and musical director, shall we call him Huw, holding court at a beach bar, is an experience that has long remained in the memory, regardless of how hard one tries to remove it!

On the previous occasion I had seen Huw, resplendent in top hat and black tails, he was supervising a burial. Now, at the Kon-Tiki Beach Bar he was imaginatively dressed for the occasion in a loud flowered shirt which, stained by sangria, was even more colourful than the manufacturer intended. He also wore Bermuda shorts that once matched the now stained shirt. Red face, straw hat, white socks and sandals and a Churchillian cigar completed the ensemble. Giorgio Armani, eat your heart out.

I am not sure what it was about the loud beer-swilling group that gave it away, but the passing 'looky looky' men seemed to realise they were British holidaymakers and regularly homed in on the group. Apart from a pair of fake Ray-Ban sunglasses, which were later blamed for Huw's headache – nothing to do with the beer, very little was bought or sold.

Their courage suitably boosted by an afternoon on the beer, a few of the boys decided to "give this windsurfing lark a go".

"Looks simple enough," said Gary, the intrepid deputy accompanist and trainee undertaker. Gary, David and Berwyn pooled their resources and hired a board for an hour. After a very basic and rudimentary lesson, to everyone's amazement, particularly given his lack of co-ordination with a baton, Gary managed to stand upright on the board at his first attempt. He even managed to avoid fellow windsurfers, paddling children and feuding parents as he headed confidently out to sea.

Unfortunately the aforementioned rudimentary lesson didn't include how to stop or how to turn around and by now Gary was far from confident. As he disappeared out to sea, David and Berwyn did what all close friends would do in similar circumstances. They joined Huw and the boys at the Kon-Tiki Beach Bar. After a few minutes and by now barely able to see Gary as he headed towards the horizon, Berwyn suggested they should perhaps point out his predicament to the lifeguards. Besides, as Berwyn pointed out, "if we don't get him back soon, we won't get our turn." The now angry people, who hired the windsurfer to the boys, had in fact beaten them to it.

"Leave 'im go – he's 'effin useless anyway," said Huw. "Why do you think they call 'im 'Gary Choc'? Because 'e is as much use as an 'effin chocolate fireguard."

The windsurfing company decided it was time to rescue their board (and Gary), and the inflatable speedboat was readied and dispatched to the rescue. The boys from the choir lined the water's edge. As a suitably embarrassed Gary was towed back to shore, sitting on his board, in true choir style and conducted by Huw (the sangria splattered undertaker), the boys treated the bemused onlookers to their rendition of,

'Show him the way to go home – he's tired and he wants to go to bed'.

By breakfast the following morning, Gary had become a bit of a celebrity and someone had christened him Thor, after Thor Heyerdahl, the Norwegian adventurer who had crossed the Pacific Ocean in a self-made raft, ironically named Kon-Tiki.

"After the beach bar?" asked Gary Choc, aka Thor.

"Bore da. Tidy breakfast," said Huw, now wearing a less colourful shirt – the sangria stains having been replaced on this particular Polynesian creation by a smattering of tomato sauce from the breakfast beans. "Let's go see the venue."

Huw went on ahead in a taxi to check out the venue, accompanied by choir stage manager Iorwerth, Gary Choc (deputy MD and the choir's windsurfing champion), plus Linda the accompanist, christened 'The Lovely Linda' by Huw.

I arrived at the venue barely ten minutes after the advance party, but in plenty of time for Huw to have provoked his first argument of the day. It was, of course, a misunderstanding brought about by the fact that Huw's Spanish was nonexistent and Pepe the caretaker's English was of a similar standard. Huw, Gary and Iorwerth attempted to move the grand piano a few metres to where Huw and Linda would like it to be on the night. Caretaker Pepe called after them. Not, as Huw thought to prevent them from moving the piano, but a) to offer help and b) to ask Huw to put out his ever present cigar.

It seems the exchange went something like this (we'll translate Pepe's Spanish… and Huw's English):

Pepe: "No smoking señor – wait one moment please, I'll help you."

Huw: pointing to his left, "Pedro, you is not stoppin' us. We is moving it over there."

Pepe: "No problem sir, but please no smoking."

Huw: still pointing to his left, "Look Pedro, I don't care wot you is saying, I am moving it there and I will have 30 blokes 'ere in ten minutes to help."

I think at this moment Huw had forgotten he was not in his Welsh Valley. I'd just left the 30 blokes in question and most of them were sleeping by the hotel pool. None of them showed any inclination to rush to Huw's aid. Indeed, apart from it being much quieter than usual, I doubt they had even noticed Huw's absence.

Pepe: by now in front of Huw, "Yes but you can't smoke anywhere, not even over there," pointing in the direction Huw had been indicating with his cigar.

With his lit cigar still in his left hand, Huw was gesticulating wildly.

At this moment I arrived in time to see an exasperated Pepe snatch the cigar from a visibly shaken Huw and then, alone, physically move the piano to exactly where Huw wanted it.

Huw: "*Gracias* Pedro, but if you wanted a smoke all you 'ad to do was ask."

Pepe: "*Di Nada*" (It's nothing).

Twenty minutes later, piano shifted, staging in place, the lovely Linda had practised a couple of the songs for the evening concert. So, along with and Iorwerth and Gary Choc, she made for the café/bar.

"I'll be along in 15 minutes," said Huw. At that moment, I was standing unseen at the back of the theatre with Pepe. Huw, a wonderful musician, sat at the piano and played beautifully for ten minutes solely for his own pleasure.

"*Un buen hombre*," said Pepe, "a good man".

"Oi, but," shouts Huw. "I know you is there now, sneaky bugger. Tidy instrument that, but it needs shifting back. Let's 'ave a beer first and bring Pedro. Tell 'im it's my shout and he can 'ave a beer and cadge one of my fags."

The concert that night was a notable success and an audience of several hundred contributed several thousand

Euros to local charities. At the start of the evening I stood backstage with Huw and the choristers. The choristers marched on and Huw and Linda waited to be introduced by the MC. Huw, of course, had heard all the undertaker jokes a thousand times and as the MC again used the same lines to introduce Huw, Huw took a swift nip from his flask and from behind the curtain flicked several imaginary 'V' signs at the MC before marching on to stand before his excellent choir.

"Was 'e flickin' his Vs?" asked MC Emyr? "Thinks I don't know," he continued as I looked puzzled. "I tells the same jokes just to wind 'im up."

By the way, in keeping with the funeral theme of this chapter, the lovely Linda was not only lovely but very blonde and she played the organ at the local crematorium. It was often quite disconcerting as I stood in line to file past the coffin as it descended into the flames to see lovely blonde Linda offering a discreet wave and a wink.

One such funeral was old Jack's. Jack had been a prisoner of war of the Germans and, having tried and failed to escape on several occasions, had spent much of his incarceration in the punishment cells.

Not surprisingly, almost 60 years later, Jack still wasn't too keen on the Germans and would voice his opinion to anyone who cared to listen. Indeed when the choir proposed a trip to Dortmund, Jack convinced them that they shouldn't go and their time would be better spent in Liverpool where they could at least support the struggling dockers!

To be fair, it wasn't an irrational hatred of all Germans. It was the Nazis Jack hated. He wouldn't travel to Mussolini's Italy or even to Franco's Spain. Indeed Berndt, a German member of the choir, could often be found in Jack's company in the bar after choir practice.

"New generation see," Jack would explain. Berndt and Jack would talk for hours and for anyone privileged to be in on one of their conversations it was extremely interesting.

Berndt's grandfather would possibly have fought against Jack's generation, if not personally against Jack.

At Jack's funeral the choir sang emotionally to a packed church, before singing again at an equally packed crematorium. Berndt sang as emotionally and as proudly as anyone, probably more so and with a tear in his eye. 'Calon Lân' was a favourite of old Jack as, of course, was 'The Red Flag'. The *coup de grâce* though came right at the end. As the eulogy finished and old Jack's coffin slowly disappeared into the flames, audience and choir each looked at the person next to them as Bud Flannigan's theme tune to *Dad's Army* and homage to the Home Guard bade Jack farewell.

'Who do you think you are kidding, Mr Hitler.

If you think we're on the run...'

Berndt smiled... we all smiled... Linda and Huw winked as I filed past...

*

With so many professions making up the average choir, not to mention differing ages amongst the choristers, it is often difficult to find a compromise date to tour. Teachers and indeed students are restricted to school holidays, which are often the most expensive dates to travel, whilst farmers are unable to travel at certain times, such as lambing season. Grandparents are always needed for childminding duties. Self-employed builders and gardeners would generally prefer to travel in the winter when the weather at home is likely to prevent them working. The glamorous Linda, choir accompanist and eye candy, can only take her holidays when her deputy is available to replace her, while 'Pete the Pill', the local chemist, is a popular member of his choir and as such is a compulsory tourist, so it is a good job he has someone to replace him in the shop.

While undertakers are an integral part of many choirs, it

is true to say that all walks of life are represented in a choir: tinker, tailor, soldier, sailor, rich man, poor man, beggar man, thief (?), butcher, baker, candlestick maker, serving all areas of the community. In most cases, as choristers' age, we can prefix most of the occupations with an ex-: ex-butcher, ex-baker and, of course, ex-miner.

At practice and in concerts, the barrister stands next to the builder, the bank manager next to the unemployed factory worker, the teacher next to the truant. In larger city choirs it is often only when the choir 'goes on tour' that one gets to know the man who you stand next to at choir. This is why many newer choirs see touring as a bonding experience.

However, in most villages, the choir can be said to be an integral part of the community. Indeed, as a number of those who have kindly contributed to this book have mentioned, the choir is like a small community. Whatever needs doing, someone from the choir will be able to do it, or will know someone who knows someone who can do it, whatever *it* is!

Choristers look after each other and for some the choir is almost like a comfort blanket, a haven where the lonely chorister can find friendship and companionship, comradeship even, when perhaps these life essentials might be missing through bereavement or divorce. For some the choir becomes the very centre of their existence. Loneliness is a desperate feeling and some people live for practice and concert nights when they can meet friends and feel important again.

There is a common theory which suggests that as choristers age and pass away, the traditional male voice choir is slowly dying, particularly in Wales. In some cases this is possibly the case. Certainly some of the more traditional larger male voice choirs are reduced in numbers from their heyday, whilst some of the smaller valleys or village choirs may have amalgamated or no longer exist.

The counter argument, however, is the proliferation of new young choirs that are being formed in Wales. Male voice, mixed voice, ladies' and youth choirs are suddenly becoming popular again and that should only be good. New choirs are being formed, but I have noticed and been reliably informed that this is mainly concentrated in the cities, especially Cardiff and perhaps London.

This might be true, but why is this?

One theory is that as the young people of Wales who were brought up in the Welsh Eisteddfod movement move from their villages and valleys to the cities in pursuit of a career, they take with them their cultural roots and meet up with other like-minded people and form a choir. Of course it is not quite as simple as that, but there is more than an element of truth in this theory. The new city choirs can only be good news for Wales and Welsh culture and certainly good for people in the cities.

The worry is that as the young people leave the valleys and villages and take their culture to the cities, and as the age of the village population increases, who actually remains in the village/valleys to maintain the culture for future generations?

My opinion is that Welsh choirs are now speaking, or should that read singing, from a position of greater strength than perhaps at any time in the last 20 years. I further believe that the same applies to our culture in general, to our singers and dancers, our poets and playwrights, our actors and performers, our producers and film-makers.

To end my political broadcast, I would say that in Wales we should perhaps utilise our culture to attract inward tourism and investment. The strength of a small nation rests with its people, its language and its culture, but do we do enough to promote our culture outside Wales? Should we do more, and if so, how should we do more? The choirs, musicians and dancers mentioned in this book certainly do, but Wales has a great cultural heritage and should perhaps make sure that we share it with the rest of the world.

For example, an argument could certainly be made that says Welsh dancing, at its best, is equally as exciting and the steps equally as intricate, if not more so than that of Irish dancing. Yet, Irish dancing is known throughout the world, whilst Welsh dancing is relatively unheard of outside Wales and the Eisteddfod movement. Why is this? Are we a little insular as a nation? We are certainly not shy. Well, Michael Flatley and his management team had something to do with the Irish phenomenon but, in the absence of a Dai Flatley, perhaps we could at least be a little more proactive when it comes to promoting our culture overseas,

Even our choirs are not necessarily the global brand some Welsh people might think. Wales – the land of song? Well perhaps Wales might be known for its singers and choirs throughout the UK and in parts of the USA and Canada and even Australia and New Zealand. Ironically, for a nation with perhaps the oldest surviving language in Europe, it is the countries where English is widely spoken that Welsh choirs are best known, whereas in mainland Europe my impression is that Wales and choirs do not necessarily go hand in hand. If one takes Patagonia out of South America, how well known are Welsh choirs in the rest of Argentina, Brazil, Chile, or in Bolivia and the remainder of the continent, or in the Spanish- and Portuguese-speaking world in general? Would the man in a Montevideo street feel that Wales is synonymous with choral music? I doubt it.

The major population centres of Africa, India, China, Russia, South America – yes our choirs have visited each of the continents, but for one to say Wales is known throughout the world for its choirs is perhaps an exaggeration... a bit of a myth, even. This is a debate which definitely needs to be continued.

CHAPTER 10

On a Personal Note

I HAVE BEEN a coach driver for a number of years, sometimes more years than I care to remember. I regularly drive schoolchildren and students, rugby and football clubs and their supporters, and generally groups of all shapes, sizes, ages and genders. I enjoy taking choirs on tour, as I am able to get to know the people and feel a part of the tour, especially if we are away for a weekend or perhaps even longer.

I especially enjoy winding up male voice choirs by playing the CDs of their nearest rival choir almost as soon as we leave Wales, or sometimes first thing on the first morning of the tour.

The banter with the choirs is a part of the job I enjoy and I even quite like it if a retired bus driver takes me to one side to tell me where I am going wrong. It doesn't happen too often!

Ladies' choirs can be as riotous as male choirs. I am often told, "If he can go off playing golf with his mates, I can go on tour with the girls." Great!

Do I have a favourite choir moment? I wouldn't like to say, but pulling up outside Mam's house with a bus load of Australian choristers who promptly sang 'Happy Birthday to Mam' is a wonderful memory that sums up choirs. Good job Mam was in. It was a complete surprise and something we had only thought of over breakfast that morning.

(Mike Digby – Coach Driver)

*

A choir is made up of people from all walks of life and those who join a choir immediately become part of a team. In the case of some choirs, part of the 'choir family'. Indeed the 'choir family' can provide a great support network.

Performing and entertaining are important reasons for joining a choir, but so too is the spirit and camaraderie one finds in a close knit choir. The support network the choir can provide should never be underestimated. At the very least, choirs can provide friendship and companionship, and even a focus for those most in need. For example, for those who are new to an area, or for those who might feel alone at times of bereavement, or when one is in the midst of the breakdown of a relationship. It is at these times that a choir can provide invaluable support.

Although a choir requires, demands even, a level of commitment and discipline from its members, most choirs also have an active social life and it is wonderful to spend time with friends. As I tell the choir, we are all in this together. We are a team. I am just the one at the front, wiggling my bottom and waving my arms around.

(Anne Wheldon – Musical Director, Côr Merched Persain)

*

One woman in charge of 40 male singers? I must be mad. Undoubtedly I must have been out of my mind when I decided during Easter 1996 that it would be a good idea to form a choir to compete in the folk competition of the National Eisteddfod of Wales, held that year in my home town – Llandeilo. I certainly had my work cut out at the time as, after gathering together a few local men, I realised that I didn't know if they could sing in tune, let alone read any music. To my astonishment and delight we were placed second out of ten competing choirs. Maybe it was beginners luck, but the dye was cast.

After winning a few times as a folk choir, my next step into the relative unknown came when I decided I needed a new challenge and, in another moment of madness, I started to develop the choir as a male voice choir and for my sins, 18 years later, I am still at it.

To be serious for a moment, the choir does play a very important part in my life and in the lives of the choristers, our families and, I hope, the town. One needs the patience of a saint at times, along with a good sense of humour and I think the boys would agree. I do consider the 'boys' not only members of my choir, but also very good friends. As such, the social aspect of the choir is as important as the singing, perhaps more so for some.

Basically Bois y Castell is a group of men who love singing and what could be better than to have a woman in charge?

(Nia Clwyd, Musical Director, Bois y Castell, Llandeilo)

*

Born in Milan to a Welsh father and an Italian mother who now lives in Cardiff, surely I was destined to become one of the great tenors? Reality soon dawned and I opted for the next best thing. I donated my average tenor voice to male voice choir singing!

Over the subsequent 40 years I have become a bit of a fanatic and this wonderful pastime has given me lifelong friendships and allowed me to help raise considerable amounts for very deserving causes. How else could an average tenor get to sing at the Royal Albert Hall and the Millennium Stadium, Cardiff, amongst many other prestigious venues?

I joined Carlton Male Voice Choir in 1982 and as I was

teaching history at the time someone suggested I become the choir historian. Simple choir logic really. Somehow, along the way, I also became choir compere. I have recently become choir chairman and I am determined to recognize and celebrate our proud history whilst striving to safeguard the choir's future by encouraging younger guys to join the choir.

By the way, I am still a top tenor, but alas still not world class.

Rick Morrish (Chairman, compere and top tenor,
Carlton MVC and occasional top tenor with
Pendyrus Male Voice Choir.)

*

Myself and choirs

It was not until I arrived at college, Royal Holloway University of London, that the choral ideal was really thrown at me. Although I had competed as a soloist and in choirs at the Urdd Eisteddfod as a child, I had hardly sung seriously for years, because my voice, when it broke, went so deep that I didn't feel I could use it. However, within my first week of University I had performed the Rachmaninov *Vespers* with a choir, in Russian, after only three rehearsals.

The next term, Mozart's 'Requiem' followed with the college symphony orchestra. By my second year I was musical director of the college production of *Company* by Stephen Sondheim and a trusted member of the Musical Theatre Society. This was the first time I had experienced, first-hand, the variety of music accessible to the adult voice in a mixed choir.

Harmony had been drilled into me from an early age as I'd sit and listen to the four-part hymns being sung weekly in chapel, but this was the first time where I was integral to the harmony. And, to think, I had almost given up on my voice!

This was about the time when Summerhome Concert Tours crossed my path for the second time. (The first time was when, as a 17 year old, I accompanied Adran Penrhyd, a Welsh folk dancing group on a tour to Spain.) Once again in Torrevieja, I was invited along with Christine Brown, a young soprano, to accompany a visiting Welsh choir. As the choir was from my home town, I could hardly refuse, but what I will never forget from that tour was being invited to the home of a local classical singer and musician, Alba, for 'wine and a musical discussion'.

Christine and I arrived at Alba's home with a bottle of wine and perhaps a certain apprehension, wondering what the next 30 minutes would entail.

Three hours later, having experienced Spanish hospitality first-hand and finished a second bottle of wine with some wonderful homemade tapas, we left Alba's home having had a remarkably wide discussion on music from all eras and continents.

Christine and I were taught a local lullaby by Alba. Nothing made me happier than seeing Alba's face with tears rolling down her cheeks, as we performed my arrangement of that very lullaby at our concert the following night. Music really is a universal language!

I had wonderful friends at college who were singers and organists who kept me close to my classical choral roots. So, when I finished college and rediscovered my voice, I knew that I had something to offer. I also realised the social advantages of being involved with such groups.

I moved to Cardiff in 2005 and, with very few friends in the area, I was looking for something to do from a musical and social perspective. On a chance night out I bumped into Eilir Owen Griffiths whom I had met earlier in the summer whilst playing seven-a-side soccer for a S4C team against the

Urdd (that institution keeps popping up!) and I was invited along to a rehearsal with his choir – CF1. By the way, if you had seen me playing football, you would know why I am a musician.

Within a few months I was an official accompanist with the choir and now I am deputy conductor. As such I am arranging and composing pieces for the choir. I have been introduced to such a wide array of people whom I now call friends. It's not only a choir, it is almost a community in its own right. The opportunities that have arisen from being part of the choir are endless.

Competition and travel have been vital in bringing people together. The choir has had many successes on the national stage and this has brought great musical experiences. When touring such places as New York, Chicago, Pennsylvania, Toronto, Niagara, Warsaw and Cork, there is something special in achieving a goal en masse, especially when everyone works so hard to attain the high standard required. The old adage of 'work hard, play hard' could not be truer.

I have also discovered that choirs are better than any dating agency. I am lucky enough to be dating Rhiannon, the choir's other, prettier accompanist; however, on the last count there are nine couples within CF1. As we grow older the choir baby count is increasing, which has to be good for future generations of choristers, assuming we don't run out of babysitters. There's also many an interesting tale of drunken liaisons which shall not be revealed.

More recently I have been introduced to a whole new aspect of the choir – conducting! In September 2010 I was invited to take over as musical director of the Cardiff Blues Choir (Côr y Gleision).

For the first time I found myself standing in front of 60 people who had little or no singing experience and who had a repertoire of around ten rugby songs and a few Welsh classics. The work and effort that the choir has put in since I joined has been incredible. We have completely transformed the repertoire, winning the mixed voice class at the North Wales Choral Festival and also at the Cheltenham Festival of Performing Arts. We also toured Torrevieja in August 2012; sadly we didn't meet up with Alba. Incredible, in just over two years the choir number has increased to over 100.

The choir has given me the outlet to put my creative juices to the test, and we are not talking about the aforementioned baby stakes here. My compositional output is greater than it has ever been and now choirs from all over Wales and beyond are singing and more importantly enjoying my pieces.

To sum up, I suppose you can never pinpoint exactly how you end up doing anything in life, but if I were to be honest, I would say that without a choir and a love of music, I certainly wouldn't be where I am today.

Despite rumours to the contrary, choral music is alive and well and living in Wales... and in many other places!

> Richard Vaughan (Musical Director Côr y Gleision, composer, pianist, conductor and music historian.)

*

Craig has cerebral palsy and is diabetic. Despite this, Craig has a terrific sense of humour and is fiercely determined not only to lead a full and active life, but also to contribute to our choir. On one occasion, after a four-hour journey from Melbourne, we arrived at the concert venue, an old country church, which on this occasion was packed to the rafters with an expectant audience. However, on arrival, our first concern was how to get our blind chorister, Kristian, and several elderly choristers up the long, winding dark staircase that led to what I call the 'minstrel gallery', where we were to be seated and, of course, we wanted to know how Craig could get there too. A discussion with his father resulted, much to his and the choristers amusement, in Craig reversing up the staircase on his backside. He approached the task with his usual determination and the ever present grin that makes Craig such a well-liked and valued member of the choir. I must say that on this occasion, coming down the stairs in much the same way as he went up might have resulted in a pain in the a**e!

By the way if you who were fortunate enough to attend the 2012 festival of 1,000 voices at the MEN Arena, Manchester, you would have noticed Craig. He was the chorister with the big beaming grin... and the wheelchair.

*

Getting Kristian up the aforementioned dark winding staircase was not too much of a hardship. Kristian is blind so the dark obviously didn't bother him at all. My stumbling over the stairs and almost dragging him down might have concerned him.

Kristian has been an integral part of the choir since 1998 and is a bit of a larrikin. He is blessed with a lovely voice, a remarkable memory and a wicked sense of humour. Many years ago I was foolish enough to teach him a rugby song. This particular version kicks off with the words, 'The Mayor of Bayswater, he has a lovely daughter'. Since learning the song Kristian is wont to tease me by starting to sing the song at the most inappropriate moments, for example as we are walking into a church or a cathedral.

During the singing of the Lord's Prayer, just before the 'trespassers' section, Kristian will often start to quietly giggle as he threatens to sing 'lead us Snot into temptation'. He never does, of course. Just like the Mayor's lovely daughter, he just does it to wind us up. It works every time.

When the choir appeared at the Sydney Opera House, I asked Kristian if he needed the toilet, to which he answered that he did. Knowing how he takes care of his ablutions, I took Kristian to the toilet, hoping to put him into a cubicle. Unfortunately, there was a queue, so I had no option but to put Kristian in front of a urinal. Kristian drops everything to the floor! I stood facing the door with my body shielding him, desperately trying to save his dignity. Or was it my dignity I was trying to save?

During our 2012 UK tour our rehearsal finished early which meant his parents, who had slipped out for a bite to eat, were not yet back to accompany Kristian to his room. We went to reception where they seemed to be having difficulty locating his key, or even his room number? "Come on," I said, "Let's go. I am sure we'll find your room." To which Kristian responded, "Uncle Neil, it's a bit like the blind, leading the blind".

Neil Kinsey (Australian Welsh Male Choir)

Joke from the Coach III

A N AUSTRALIAN CHORISTER on a tour of England and Wales wanders into a magnificent church in central London.

Taking his time to explore this beautiful church and to soak up the atmosphere of a building that was approximately 400 years older than his country, our chorister, Bruce, noticed an old red telephone box just inside the rear door of the church. Curious, Bruce read the sign on the telephone box and was astounded to see that it was £10,000 per call.

Taken aback, Bruce sought out the vicar and asked why it was such an expensive call.

"Ah, my son," replied the vicar. Ten thousand pounds will offer you a direct line to the Almighty, to God".

Slightly puzzled, but otherwise content with the explanation, Bruce jumped on a red London bus and was soon with his friends from the choir.

Next stop for the choir was Oxford as they were due to sing at a beautiful old church in a nearby village. Some of the gravestones in the cemetery bore dates that were nearly 300 years older than his adopted country, even older than some of the choristers in his choir, Bruce chuckled to himself. Then, at the entrance to the church, he spied a telephone. To his amazement a sign above the telephone read: "£10,000 per call."

One of the local choristers introduced Bruce to the choirmaster who, in turn, explained to Bruce that for £10,000, one could indeed find a direct line to God.

And so the tour of England continued, Birmingham, Worcester, Bath and finally Bristol. Everywhere he visited

Bruce found a beautiful old church and in each church was a telephone with a sign which read: £10,000 per call.

And so to Wales – 'The Land of Song'. As the bus crossed the Severn Bridge, Bruce, obviously a sensitive man of some refinement, swore he could hear choirs singing and music being played. Of course, it was more likely to be the aftereffects of the choir's 'farewell to England' evening in Bristol.

On the choir's first night in Wales, our Australian friends were entertained by a Welsh choir, along with folk musicians and dancers.

The following morning Bruce felt a bit sore. He should never have tried the dance with the broomstick, but otherwise he was happy and looking forward to his tour of Mumbles and the Gower Peninsula. Bruce had read that the Gower Peninsula was the first area of Britain to be designated an area of outstanding natural beauty, and looking around the Gower, he certainly wasn't disappointed.

Bruce came across a lovely little church, probably older than anything he had seen in England. Bruce opened the door and went inside. Lo and behold, there it was – a telephone! Approaching the telephone, he read the sign. But what's this? Bruce reached for his glasses and… sure enough, the sign read: "50 pence per call."

Urgently seeking out the elderly vicar, Bruce asked the question and was reassured by the priest, who actually looked older than Bruce's adopted country, that yes, the sign was correct and for 50p one could have a direct line to God.

"Why only 50 pence per call?" Bruce respectfully asked the vicar." In England the same call costs £10,000?"

"Indeed," said the gentle vicar, "but don't forget my son, you are in Wales now. It's a local call!"

Also from Y Lolfa:

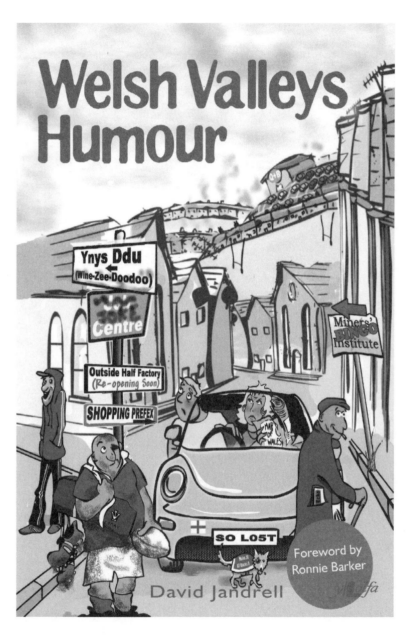

£3.95

y Lolfa

Brothers, Sing On!

A History of Pontarddulais Male Choir (1960–2010)

Eric Jones

£7.95

Welsh Choirs on Tour is just one of a whole range of publications from Y Lolfa. For a full list of books currently in print, send now for your free copy of our new full-colour catalogue. Or simply surf into our website

www.ylolfa.com

for secure on-line ordering.

TALYBONT CEREDIGION CYMRU SY24 5HE
e-mail ylolfa@ylolfa.com
website www.ylolfa.com
phone (01970) 832 304
fax 832 782